THE LAST MEETING OF THE KNIGHTS OF THE WHITE MAGNOLIA

A PLAY IN TWO ACTS
BY PRESTON JONES

(One of the three plays comprising A TEXAS TRILOGY)

DRAMATISTS PLAY SERVICE INC.

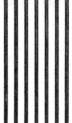

THE LAST MEETING OF THE KNIGHTS OF THE WHITE MAGNOLIA
Copyright © 1973, 1976, Preston Jones

All Rights Reserved

SPECIAL NOTE

To my beloved wife, Mary Sue

THE LAST MEETING OF THE KNIGHTS OF THE WHITE MAGNOLIA was first presented in New York City by Robert Whitehead and Roger L. Stevens (as one of three full-length plays in repertory collectively entitled A TEXAS TRILOGY*) at the Broadhurst Theatre on September 22, 1976. It was directed by Alan Schneider; the scenery and lighting were by Ben Edwards; and the costumes were by Jane Greenwood. The assistant director was Joan Thorne. The cast, in order of appearance, was as follows:

RAMSEY-EYES .... John Marriott

RUFE PHELPS .... Walter Flanagan

OLIN POTTS .... Thomas Toner

RED GROVER .... Patrick Hines

L. D. ALEXANDER .... Henderson Forsythe

SKIP HAMPTON .... Graham Beckel

COLONEL J. C. KINKAID .... Fred Gwynne

LONNIE ROY MCNEIL .... Paul O'Keefe

MILO CRAWFORD .... Josh Mostel

TIME AND PLACE: Bradleyville, Texas, 1962
Meeting room of the "Knights of the White Magnolia" on the third floor of the Cattleman's Hotel

* Consisting of THE LAST MEETING OF THE KNIGHTS OF THE WHITE MAGNOLIA, LU ANN HAMPTON LAVERTY OBERLANDER and THE OLDEST LIVING GRADUATE

Author's Note

An extraordinary energy in the theater is the energy of the playwright. It tells us things. It gives us life as no other element of theater can. It is relentless and often difficult. So, pay attention.

PAUL BAKER

For a playwright, there can be no greater thrill than to see his plays first come to life on the stage. Therefore, I look back with special fondness to the fall of 1973 when the Dallas Theater Center began work on *A Texas Trilogy*. As a member of the Theater Center since 1962, I had come to appreciate the hard work and lively creativity that surround each production. This became especially clear to me when the trilogy plays were produced under the direction of Paul Baker.

The Dallas Theater Center has a tradition of producing original plays because Paul Baker is committed to supporting the playwright on both artistic and economic levels. My plays, and those of other writers, have grown out of this nourishing atmosphere, one which encourages each new play to find its way.

Rehearsals for *A Texas Trilogy* were creative enterprises involving everyone. Lines were added and cut, plots were strengthened. Schemes were devised to help actors understand the social and environmental aspects of Bradleyville. In order to deepen their characterizations, actors were asked to construct collages designed to capture, in textural forms, the basic elements of each character's past life. These and other techniques used throughout rehearsals of the three plays were valuable and stimulating to all of us—director, designer, actors, and playwright alike.

For this enriching experience I am grateful to Paul Baker, Eugene McKinney, Randy Moore, Ken Latimer, Sallie Laurie, Mona Pursley, Robyn Flatt, James Crump, John Henson, Synthia Rodgers, John Logan, Tim Green, William Landrey, Allen Hibbard, Tommy Kendrick, Ted

Mitchell, Sam Nance, Keith Dixon, Chris McCarty, Charles Beachley, Roger Richards, Matt Tracy, and Rebecca Ramsey. I wish to acknowledge my appreciation to these fine artists and true first citizens of ' Bradleyville.

The Last Meeting of the Knights of the White Magnolia was first performed at the Down Center Stage of the Dallas Theater Center on December 4, 1973. Two months later, on February 5, 1974, *Lu Ann Hampton Laverty Oberlander* premiered at the same theater. Then, beginning on November 19, 1974, with *The Oldest Living Graduate*, all three plays were produced in repertory on the Dallas Theater Center's main stage, the Kalita Humphreys Theater. Performances were under the direction of Paul Baker and cast from the resident company and graduate apprentices at the Dallas Theater Center.

The Last Meeting of the Knights of the White Magnolia was chosen by the American Playwrights Theatre as its 1975-76 offering, and the play has been produced by numerous regional, university, civic, and professional theaters across the country.

Starting on April 29, 1976, the John F. Kennedy Center for the Performing Arts presented *A Texas Trilogy* in repertory at its Eisenhower Theater in Washington, D.C. The plays, which ran for a ten-week season under the direction of Alan Schneider, were produced by Robert Whitehead and Roger L. Stevens. On August 5, 1976, the trilogy was brought back to the Kennedy Center for a five-week run prior to its New York opening.

The Place

Bradleyville, Texas—population 6,000—a small, dead West Texas town in the middle of a big, dead West Texas prairie between Abilene and San Angelo. The new highway has bypassed it and now the world is trying to.

The People

THE HAMPTON FAMILY

CLAUDINE HAMPTON attended high school in Bradleyville and, through a program at the hospital, became a practical nurse. She married Lloyd Hampton. Lloyd worked for the refinery until his death in 1945. Claudine has two children, Skip and Lu Ann. Both of them are grown now but still remain a great source of worry to her. Mrs. Hampton is well known in town for her ability and honesty.

SKIP HAMPTON was born and raised in Bradleyville, graduating from high school and serving in the army during the Korean War. In his entire life Skip has never been able to distinguish himself in any type of endeavor. If you look in his *Senior Year Annual* from Bradleyville High, you'll find under his picture the name Skip Hampton and nothing else. During Korea, Skip drove a supply truck—never getting closer to the front than sixty miles; however, with the passage of time and especially after many drinks, his war record gets bloodier and bloodier. After the war Skip tried several get-rich-quick schemes that always melted in his hands. Then he discovered the bottle. Skip is unmarried and lives with his mother and sister. He pumps gas for a living and has finally been able to distinguish himself in the eyes of all Bradleyville. He is the town drunk.

LU ANN HAMPTON was born at the Bradleyville Memorial Hospital in 1936. She suffered through the usual amount of bites, cuts, scratches, bruises, and minor childhood ailments, but never knew real heartbreak until her father died in 1945. Another blow came when her best friend moved to California in 1947.

Always a popular girl in school, Lu Ann held several offices. She was co-editor of the grade school *Messenger*, and member of the Pepettes drill team. In high school, she was four times elected to the student senate as the representative of Miss Scott's home room and was, in her sophomore year, Future Farmers of America Sweetheart and class yearbook reporter. She could have held many more offices, but the demanding chores of being Head Cheerleader for the past two years have forced her to curtail many activities. Lu Ann lives with her mother and brother at 301 Grand Street and goes steady with Billy Bob Wortman. After graduation from high school, she plans "to have lots and lots of fun."

CHARMAINE is Lu Ann's daughter by Dale Laverty. After Corky Oberlander was killed, Lu Ann moved back into her mother's house and Charmaine was brought up there. She is spoiled and pampered by her mother, her grandmother, and her uncle.

Charmaine became the child of an unsettled household and unsettled times. As the years passed, she grew ashamed of her mother, contemptuous of her uncle, and utterly unseeing of her invalid grandmother. Her school grades are bad, her outlook bleak, her lifestyle slovenly and wasteful, but maybe all these negatives equip her better than her mother for today's times.

BILLY BOB WORTMAN lives with his mother, father, and three younger sisters in a small house on Austin Street. Always interested in agriculture, Billy Bob has been a member of Future Farmers of America since 1947, and his entries have won many prizes at the Mumford County Fair. Now, in his senior year in high school, Billy Bob is an Eagle Scout, a Y.M.C.A. summer camp counselor, and a starting forward on the varsity basketball team.

Next to his father, Billy Bob considers Reverend Stone of the First Christian Church one of the finest men that ever lived. Billy Bob started going steady with Lu Ann Hampton at the beginning of his senior year, right after she had broken up with Floyd Tatum and he had broken up with Eveline Blair. (Ruthie Lee Lawell got them together at a sock-hop.)

Billy Bob isn't too sure what his plans are after graduation, but you can bet whatever it is, it will have something to do with basketball and the Lord.

DALE LAVERTY was born and raised in San Angelo, Texas. Always a big kid, Dale was known as Tubby Rump until he made first-string tackle on the football team and became known as the Hulk.

Dale's father was a truck driver and trucks became the passion of

Dale's life. He dreamed of them. He saw himself in the cab rolling along in his own rig, booming across the Western plains, free and easy with the girls at the brightly lit truck stops. He would dream of swinging out of the cab and eating hugely on ham and eggs, great bowls of chili, fat-dripping cheeseburgers, and chicken-fried steak swimming and bubbling in heavy gravy.

Dale would like to be the hood ornament of a Mack truck, solid, heavy, tough, staring down the road in open-eyed defiance.

After the Korean War, in which he served as a truck driver, Dale came home with great goals in mind. He wished for a wife, a trailer house, a new Chevy, and a job driving semis. Man's needs are simple and his wants are few, but his lusts are strong and of great variety.

CORKY OBERLANDER was born into a German Lutheran family on a cotton farm outside Roscoe, Texas. He graduated from high school and served a hitch in the army engineers. Afterward, he returned home and used his army-learned surveying skills to get a job with the Highway Department in Abilene.

In 1959, Corky married Peggy Sue Roberts from Sweetwater. The marriage lasted only a few short months before she ran off with a core drill operator. (Peggy Sue always was about half-wild.) After the divorce, Corky spent a weekend getting drunk and laid in Juarez, Mexico. Then he stoically went back to work.

Corky likes to fish, hunt, play softball, and drink a few beers. He was having a few beers when he found himself at Red Grover's bar in Bradleyville and met a young lady named Lu Ann Hampton Laverty.

TOWN FOLK

L. D. ALEXANDER grew up in Bradleyville and married his high-school sweetheart. After his return from World War II, L.D. went to work for A.B.C. Supermarkets, Inc. He soon rose to the rank of manager, a modest but respectable position in Bradleyville's middle-class society. L.D. has two children, a boy and a girl. L.D. believes in white supremacy. L.D. is the guy with the green apron and the tag that says MGR. He is usually standing around the checkout stand.

RAMSEY-EYES BLANKENSHIP has lived in Bradleyville since he was ten years old and has known the secondhand existence of a West Texas black. In his own world, he is simply known as Granddaddy; in the white world he is Ramsey-Eyes. His full name, Ramsey Washington Blankenship has been used twice—once when he was baptized and once when he was married. It will not be used again until his funeral. Since the death of his wife, Ramsey-Eyes has lived by himself in a small, sagging, three-room house. Most of his children have moved to bigger cities and his grandchildren upset him with their mutterings about social change. As long as Ramsey-Eyes can earn his keep and go fishing every weekend, then he is content. He moves through his old age like a shuffling shadow.

MILO CRAWFORD was born and raised in Bradleyville. He was five years old when his father died, and Milo, an only child, came under his mother's grip. After graduating from high school, Milo was spared the draft when his mother claimed he was her sole support. For many years now Milo has worked at the Bradleyville Grain and Feed Store. Milo has contemplated marriage now and again, but the thought of leaving Mama is too painful for him to get seriously involved with a bride-to-be. Milo has made two great decisions in his life without consulting Mama: one, to take up cigarette smoking, and the other, to join the Knights of the White Magnolia, both decisions being mild forms of rebellion. To counteract these moves, Mama hides the ashtrays and tries to think up little errands for him to run on meeting nights.

RED GROVER is originally from Meridian, Mississippi. Red came to Bradleyville following its brief oil boom right after World War II, a conflict he served in totally without distinction. When the "homecoming G.I.'s" defeated the Baptists in the local "wet, dry election," Red took his savings and put up Red's Place, a bar and package liquor store. When the boom had run itself out and the wells were capped, Red found himself shunned by most of the townspeople and, like most bar owners, developed a deep disgust for his clients. Never taking a wife, Red rides out his sexual desires on skinny-legged barmaids and drunken divorcees and grows more and more bitter as the days and nights drag on.

RUFE PHELPS as a young man worked in various oil fields around West Texas. However, after he married, he settled down to a more permanent position at the refinery.

OLIN POTTS grew up on a family farm and stayed there. He married late in life and lives out at his place with his wife and mother. Olin and

Rufe are both childless and have kept up a competitive struggle that began in grade school. They went through their softball and rodeo stage and are now hard at each other at checkers, fishing, dove hunting, horseshoes, and dominoes. Their ages and occupations kept them out of World War II and they spent the war years running trotlines and betting on the outcome of battles.

MIKE TREMAINE has lived in Bradleyville all his life. He is married and has three children. Mike grows watermelon and cotton on a small farm outside of town. He also works as general handyman for Floyd Kinkaid and has done so for about a year.

THE KINKAID FAMILY

COLONEL J. C. KINKAID is old and confined to a wheelchair. He was born in 1887 on his father's ranch, and in his youth he enjoyed the soft life that a cattle and cotton empire could provide. In his later years the God of Fortune that looks down on and loves us all added a further bonanza to him in the form of oil wells. He attended high school at Mirabeau B. Lamar Military Academy and went on to Texas A&M, choosing a military career over ranch life. The Colonel served with General John Pershing in the Philippines, in Mexico, and finally in France during World War I. What started out to be a fulfilling military career in the Philippines ended in the trenches in France. "The Colonel returned from the great war to continue in his family's business interests in and around Bradleyville, Texas, and is interested in many civic organizations," or so his paragraph reads in the *Texas Who's Who*. Actually, the Colonel returned from France shattered in mind and body. Luckily for the family, an older brother kept the fortune together until the Colonel's son Floyd took up his father's half of the business and simply let the Colonel ramble on into his lost world of memories. Now in his dotage, the Colonel's string is starting to run out.

FLOYD KINKAID is a power in this small town and he knows it. Floyd's interests are many and his hobbies are expensive: registered quarter horses, a big flashy bass boat, charter membership in the country club. He was twice president of the Jaycees and is a leading figure in all civic organizations. Floyd and his older brother, Franklin, were both born in

Bradleyville after the Colonel's return from World War I. They attended Bradleyville High and both graduated from college—Franklin from Texas A&M and Floyd from Texas Tech. When World War II broke out, Franklin went into the air force and Floyd joined the navy. Franklin was killed when his B-17 crashed in Florida, and Floyd wound up attached to a headquarters section in San Diego. After the war, Floyd married Maureen and returned to Bradleyville to take control of his father's business interests. Floyd and his Uncle Brewster Kinkaid have turned the Kinkaid holdings into a sizable money-making venture. Now, with the business virtually running itself, Floyd is becoming bored and is casting about for other interests.

MAUREEN KINKAID was born in Bradleyville of a moderately well-to-do family. She graduated from Bradleyville High and went on to Texas Tech, majoring in secondary education. She and Floyd had dated all through high school and had planned to get married after graduating from college. However, the war changed all that. Floyd went into the navy and Maureen did her bit on the Bradleyville home front answering "V" mail and collecting tinfoil. When the war was over, she and Floyd married and set up housekeeping in town. In 1957 Floyd built the new house and they moved to their present location. They have no children. Floyd secretly blames her and she secretly blames him, but neither has bothered to find out anything for sure. Maureen wonders why she's so goddamned bored with everything.

THE SICKENGER FAMILY

MARTHA ANN SICKENGER is also a Bradleyville girl. Her family owns the grain and feed store. Martha Ann graduated from high school in 1953 and was considered at the time to be "a little bit on the wild side." After a disastrous one semester at Texas University, Martha Ann returned home and grabbed off Clarence Sickenger, much to the town's amusement, Clarence being thirty-four at the time. However, their two children, Howard and Charlotte Marie, came bouncing into being and everybody came around to admitting that it might be a pretty good match after all. Martha Ann seems to think so, and if Clarence just happens to be one of the richest men in town, well, "what the hell."

CLARENCE SICKENGER is also a lifelong Bradleyville citizen; like Floyd, he too comes from a wealthy family. He graduated from Texas University and spent World War II right in Bradleyville—exempt from the draft because of his value to the oil industry. In 1953, Clarence married Martha Ann Montgomery and they settled down to a life of small-town wealth. Although Clarence and Floyd have never been close friends, they started a conversation out at the country-club bar the other day that had the makings of a real partnership.

Characters

RAMSEY-EYES BLANKENSHIP *Seventy-five. Black custodian of the Cattleman's Hotel*

RUFE PHELPS *Fifty-five. Refinery worker*

OLIN POTTS *Fifty-six. Cotton farmer*

RED GROVER *Forty-eight. Owner of Red's Place, a small bar*

L. D. ALEXANDER *Forty-nine. Manager of A.B.C. Supermarket*

COLONEL J. C. KINKAID *Seventy-five. Colonel, U.S. Army (Ret.). Owner of Cattleman's Hotel*

SKIP HAMPTON *Thirty-one. Texaco service station attendant*

LONNIE ROY McNEIL *Twenty-one. Pipe fitter at Silver City Pipe Company*

MILO CRAWFORD *Twenty-six. Clerk at Bradleyville Grain & Feed*

THE LAST MEETING OF
THE KNIGHTS OF
THE WHITE MAGNOLIA

ACT I

The time is 1962 in Bradleyville, Texas. The setting is the meeting room of the Knights of the White Magnolia on the third floor of the Cattleman's Hotel. The plastered walls are stained and faded, the floor warped and splintered, patched here and there with flat tin cans. Chairs of various ages, colors, and styles are scattered about the room. One is an old wheelchair. At one end of the room (Stage Right) is a small podium on a low platform. On the face of the podium is painted a rather smudged white magnolia flower. On the wall behind the podium are two flags, "The Stars and Bars" and the "Lone Star," both very old and very dirty. Between the two flags hangs a cross made of light bulbs. Stage Left is the door into the room. Along the upstage wall is a coat rack. On the floor by the coat rack is an old trunk containing the initiation hats. Hanging on the Stage Left and Upstage wall are old banners representing the sun, the moon, the west wind and truth.

As the scene opens, it is early evening. Ramsey-Eyes is listlessly sweeping the floor. He is an old black man in very old clothes. As he sweeps the floor he hums and sings snatches of "Red River Valley."

After a bit we hear the voices of Rufe Phelps *and* Olin Potts. Rufe *wears khaki work clothes and a baseball cap.* Olin *wears Levi's, a cotton work shirt, and a straw hat.*

RUFE. (*Offstage.*) Ah been playin' horseshoes since Jesus H. Christ was a windmill salesman and ah never seen nuthin' like it.
OLIN. (*Offstage.*) What the hell are you talkin' about?
RUFE. (*Entering.*) Ah wouldn't play horseshoes with you again, Olin Potts, if you was the last man left in West Texas, and that's by-God fact.
RAMSEY-EYES. Howdy, Mr. Rufe, Howdy, Mr. Olin.

OLIN. (*Entering.*) Aw hell, Rufe, ah never done nuthin'.

RUFE. Never done nuthin'! Never done nuthin'! Hell, ah spoze cheatin' is nuthin'. Nuthin' to *you*, that is. No, sir, to a fella like *you*, cheatin' is jest nuthin' atall.

RAMSEY-EYES. How is you-all this evenin'?

OLIN. Now listen here, Rufe Phelps, ah never cheated!

RUFE. Never cheated! Well, ah don't know what cheatin' is if what you done *wasn't*.

RAMSEY-EYES. Shore been hot today, ain't it!?

OLIN. (*Sitting.*) Ah never cheated.

RUFE. Did it!

OLIN. Didn't!

RAMSEY-EYES. You-all is kinda early tonight, ain't you?

RUFE. That last throw of mine was a leaner.

OLIN. Weren't neither.

RUFE. Was too!

OLIN. Weren't!

RUFE. How's come it weren't?

OLIN. Cause for a leaner to be a leaner, it's gotta by Gawd lean!

RUFE. If that last throw of mine wasn't leanin' ah'd sure as hell like to know what it was doin'.

OLIN. It was lyin' flat on its butt in the dirt. That's what it was doin'.

RAMSEY-EYES. Yes, sah, horseshoes is a mighty good game, okay.

(*The door opens and* Red Grover *appears.* Red *is fat, thick-necked, and cynical. He wears a rumpled blue suit with a flowered necktie. He carries a paper bag containing four bottles of cheap bourbon.*)

RUFE. Hey, Red, when is a leaner a leaner?

RED. Who gives a damn!

RAMSEY. Howdy, Mistah Grover, how is you?

OLIN. That last toss of yours weren't no leaner no way.

RUFE. Was by Gawd too.

OLIN. Weren't.

RED. What you two monkey-nuts fightin' about now?

RUFE. My last throw over to the horseshoes was a leaner and Olin cheated and said it weren't.

OLIN. Well, it weren't.

RUFE. Wouldn't surprise me none if maybe you didn't kick it a little bit.

OLIN. Ah never kicked nuthin'. There was no way to kick nuthin' no ways, 'cause that damned horseshoe weren't leanin'.

RUFE. Was so too. You cheated!

20

OLIN. Didn't done it.

RUFE. Did too.

OLIN. Didn't!

RED. For Christ's sake, if all you two are gonna do is fight about it, why don't you quit playin'?

RUFE. Well, hell, Red, ah like to play.

RED. Play with somebody else then.

OLIN. Ain't nobody else to play with.

RAMSEY-EYES. Well, iffen you-all is gonna start on wif de meeting' here, ah'll jest go on down to de lobby. (*He exits.*)

RED. (*Hearing door close.*) Who the hell was that?

RUFE. Ramsey-Eyes, ah think.

RED. Well, goddamn, ah guess he's gittin' too uppity to talk to people any more. Ah swear, it's gittin' nowadays where by God you gotta talk to *them* first.

OLIN. That's about it.

(*The door opens and L. D. Alexander enters. L.D. is big and florid. He wears a baggy J. C. Penney Western suit, scuffed black loafers with white socks, and a small white Stetson hat.*)

L.D. Howdy, brothers.

RUFE. Howdy, L.D.

L.D. Man, it's dark in here. (*Touches switch. After general greeting*) You bring the re-freshments there, Red?

RED. You bet, L.D. (*He indicates paper bag.*) Best stock ah got in the house.

L.D. I'll bet. (*He picks a bottle out of the bag.*) Old Buzzard Puke. Yes, sir, Red, this looks like real smooth stuff.

RUFE. Old Buzzard Puke. That's a good one, ain't it, Olin?

OLIN. Shore is.

RED. Ah don't notice you-all passin' any of it up when it comes round.

L.D. Well, you can bet your butt Skip Hampton won't pass it up.

RED. Hell, Skip wouldn't pass up a drink if he had to squeeze it out of an armadillo's ass.

RUFE. Hey, ah got a good idea. Let's hide the whiskey and play like we ain't got any when Skip comes in.

RED. There ain't any place in this whole world to hide whiskey from Skip. He'd sniff it out if it wuz wrapped in lead.

RUFE. No, no. What we do, you see, is hide these-here bottles and then tell Skip that it was *his* turn to bring the re-freshments. Then he won't know. You see?

OLIN. Hey, that's a good one, Rufe.

RED. Might work at that.

OLIN. (*To Rufe.*) How'd you happen to think up a good one like that?

RUFE. Well, hell Olin, ah think of things sometimes.

(*Offstage, ad lib of Skip and Ramsey-Eyes.*)

OLIN. You ain't never thought of nuthin' affore.

RUFE. Now listen here, Olin Potts . . .

(*The door opens and Skip Hampton enters. Skip is a pale, thin, blond-headed man. He wears a greasy green Texaco uniform.*)

SKIP. Howdy, ever'body.

L.D. Well, howdy there, Skip, how's the boy?

SKIP. Pretty good.

RUFE. Hey, Skip, didn't you forgit somethin'?

SKIP. No, ah don't think so.

RED. Aw, come on now, Skip. Don't try to kid your old buddies.

SKIP. Ah ain't kiddin' nobody.

RUFE. Old Skip. Always tryin' to kid his buddies.

SKIP. Ah ain't kiddin', ah tell you. What the hell you-all talkin' about?

RED. What are we talkin' about? Well, hell's fire, boy, we're talkin' about the re-freshments.

SKIP. What about the re-freshments?

L.D. Where the hell are they?

SKIP. Ah don't know where they are.

RED. You mean to say you didn't bring them?

SKIP. Me? No, ah didn't bring nuthin'.

L.D. Well, Gawd Almighty damn!

RUFE. Now we ain't got nuthin' to drink.

SKIP. Red always brings them samples from the package store, he always does.

RED. Now, Skip. You know ah told you to pick it up for me and bring it over here for tonight's meetin'.

RUFE. Shore he did. He told you to, Skip. Didn't he, Olin?

OLIN. Shore did.

SKIP. No, you didn't, Red. Ah swear to God you never. Ah would of remembered. Hell's fire, ah'd never forgit somethin' as important as that.

L.D. Well, looks like we jest gotta do without tonight.

SKIP. No, wait. Ah'll go back and git it, Red. Ah'll jest run over to your place and pick some up!

RED. Too late now. Ah done locked up the package store.

SKIP. Well, you can open it again, can't you? Give me the key, ah'll go.

RED. You? Give *you* the key to mah hard liquor. You gotta be crazy, boy, that would be like givin' old L.D. here a Charg-a-Plate to a whorehouse.

SKIP. Well, let somebody else go then. How about Rufe here?

RUFE. Why should ah go do what you was supposed to do but forgot? (He *and* Olin *both giggle.*)

SKIP. (*Truth suddenly dawning on him.*) Whatta you guys tryin' to pull?

L.D. Well, hell, since old Skip let us down tonight, ah guess we gotta make do with this. (*He pulls out the sack.*)

RUFE. Gotcha there, Skip. We really gotcha there.

SKIP. (*Dully.*) Yeah, boy, that was a good one, okay.

OLIN. Rufe thought it up.

SKIP. (*Sarcastically.*) Damn good goin' there, Rufe. (*He reaches for the sack.*)

RED. (*Stopping him.*) Now hold on there. All us *gentlemen* wait on re-freshments til after the meetin', don't we, Skip?

SKIP. Sure, sure, oh, hell, yes.

(*The door opens and* Ramsey-Eyes *pokes his head in.*)

RAMSEY-EYES. 'Scuse me.

RED. What the hell you want, Ramsey-Eyes?

RAMSEY. Ah jest come up to say how Floyd done brought his daddy to the meetin'. He's down in de lobby now.

L.D. Okay, Ramsey-Eyes. (*The door closes.*) Rufe, you and Olin go on down and git Colonel Kinkaid.

RUFE. Okay, L.D.

(*They start to exit.*)

L.D. And be careful with him comin' up the stairs.

OLIN. We ain't never dropped him yet.

L.D. Old Colonel Kinkaid, by God, he's somethin' else, ain't he? Here he is all crippled up and almost blind, but wild horses wouldn't keep him from a lodge meetin'. No, sir.

SKIP. How old is the Colonel nowadays, L.D.?

L.D. Well, let's see, ah reckin he must be at least seventy-five.

SKIP. No kiddin'.

L.D. You bet; hell, all them Kinkaids is tough. All except Floyd, that is.

RED. Oh, that old man ain't so tough.

L.D. Hell he ain't.

RED. Well, goddamn, L.D., he's got the shell shocks, ain't he? All you gotta do is belch too loud and he starts yellin' about the Germans comin' after him.

L.D. Hell, Red, there were lots of fellers come back from that World's

23

War I with the shell shocks, and even with them he's still more of a man than that damn Floyd will ever be.

SKIP. That's the damn truth. You know, it's kind of funny what with Floyd and that gnat-titted wife of his, what's her name?

L.D. Maureen.

SKIP. Maureen, bein' the high by-God so-ciety in this-here town, why ain't Floyd ever joined our lodge?

RED. 'Cause he thinks it's a bunch of bullshit, that's why. All Floyd and old gnat-tits and the rest of the rich bastards in this town wanna do is sit around the goddamned country club and play kneesies. Floyd lets the Colonel come up here to the meetin's so's everyone can see how nice he is to his daddy. But you watch, the minute the Colonel kicks off, Floyd's gonna close this-here hotel before the carcass is cold.

L.D. Oh no, now he wouldn't do a thing like that.

RED. The hell he wouldn't. Floyd may be a bastard, but he's not a stupid bastard. You see how many payin' guests are in this-here fire trap? Probably about five. This mighta been a classy hotel way back yonder when the Colonel had it built, but that Holiday Inn out to the bypass done kicked this dump plumb outta business.

L.D. That don't mean a goddamn thing. Nobody's gonna close down this place. Hell, Red, this-here Cattleman's Hotel is a by-God landmark in this country.

RED. Oh, hell yes, the whole town of Bradleyville is a by-God landmark, but that didn't stop the state from runnin' the highway around it. Take a look down Main Street for Christ's sake, there's so many damned stores bein' boarded up that the only outfit in town that's makin' any money is the god-damned used-lumber company.

L.D. Well, ah admit that things is kindly slow but . . .

RED. Oh, you admit that, do you? (*He starts to laugh.*)

L.D. What the hell's so funny?

RED. I just happened to think, what if Floyd don't close the place down but turns it into a hotel for Coloreds only? By God, that would damn sure play hell with the old meetin' night.

(L.D. *and* Skip *stare at him.*)

L.D. Well, what the hell!

RED. Oh, I'm jest kiddin', of course. Floyd would never do nuthin' like that.

L.D. He damn sure wouldn't.

RED. (*Still amused.*) 'Course he wouldn't.

(*Offstage dialogue before* Colonel's *entrance.*)

COLONEL. (*Offstage.*) Watch what you're doin', damnit, you're not totin' a bale of alfalfa!

RUFE. (*Offstage.*) Ah'm sorry, Colonel. Confound it, Olin, hold up your part!

OLIN. (*Offstage.*) Ah am holdin' up my part. You're the one not doin' nuthin'.

RUFE. (*Offstage.*) Now listen here, Olin Potts.

COLONEL. (*Offstage.*) Shut the hell up, the both of you. Now open that damn door, Ramsey-Eyes.

RAMSEY-EYES. Yes sah, Colonel. (*He opens the door and goes to the wheelchair to arrange it.*)

(Olin and Rufe carry in the Colonel. *The Colonel is dressed in gabardine Western pants, slippers, and a faded, patched World War 1 officer's tunic. His legs are crippled and he is nearly blind.*) Ah got you chair here, Colonel Kinkaid, sah.

COLONEL. Good man, Ramsey-Eyes.

(Olin and Rufe start to ease the Colonel into the wheelchair.)

OLIN. Damnit, Rufe, be careful with his legs.

RUFE. Damnit yourself, ah know what ah'm doin'.

COLONEL. (*Settling into wheelchair.*) All right, all right, ah'm in, now git away from me, the both of you!

RUFE. Boy howdy, them steps up from the lobby is gittin' hard to climb.

RAMSEY-EYES. (*Arranging Colonel's lap robe.*) Ah'll be right down in the lobby iffen you need anythin'.

COLONEL. Right, Ramsey-Eyes, DISMISSED. (Ramsey-Eyes *doesn't move.*) What the hell you waitin' for?

RAMSEY-EYES. Is you wearin' your dentures tonight, Colonel?

COLONEL. Hell yes, ah'm wearin' my teeth. (*Points to them.*) See.

RAMSEY-EYES. You know what Floyd said 'bout wearin' your dentures.

COLONEL. Ah know what he said; now, damnit, *dismissed!*

RAMSEY-EYES. (*Exiting.*) Yes, sah, but Floyd said you gotta wear your dentures.

L.D. Howdy, Colonel Kinkaid.

COLONEL. Howdy, boys. How you-all tonight?

SKIP. Howdy, Colonel.

COLONEL. Who is it?

SKIP. Skip Hampton, Colonel.

COLONEL. Well, howdy there, Skip. How's your sister?

SKIP. She's jest fine, Colonel.

COLONEL. And your mother?

SKIP. Couldn't be better.

COLONEL. Ah used to court your Aunt Sally. Betcha didn't know that, did you?

SKIP. Yeah, Colonel, you told me.

COLONEL. Slapped mah face so hard one night it knocked me plumb outta the buckboard.

L.D. Sure, Colonel.

COLONEL. Thought for a second that damned buggy whip ah had in mah' hand was a lightnin' rod.

L.D. (*Going behind podium.*) Well, we might as well git started.

RUFE. Where's old Milo Crawford tonight?

L.D. Milo can't make it. He phoned over to the house and said he hadda take his mama over to Big Spring.

RED. Jesus Christ—wouldn't you know it.

L.D. (*Banging on podium with his hand.*) Okay now. This-here meetin' of the Bradleyville, Texas, Lodge of the Knights of the White Magnolia is now in order. Ever'body 'cept the Colonel stand up and repeat the oath.

ALL. (*In a rather ragged cadence.*) "Ah swear as a true Knight of the White Magnolia to preserve the merits handed to me by mah forefathers and to hold as a sacred trust the ideals of mah Southern heritage. Ah pledge mah life to the principles of White Magnolia-ism and will obey until ah die the laws of this-here so-ciety."

L.D. Okay, ever'body can sit down now. (Olin *starts to the door.*) Where the hell you goin', Olin?

OLIN. (*Surprised.*) Ah'm goin' on out to git the card tables so's we can commence with the domino games.

L.D. Well, you can jest sit on back down, 'cause we ain't havin' no dominoes tonight.

OLIN. No dominoes? What kinda meetin' can we have with no dominoes?

COLONEL. Damnit, ah wanna shuffle dominoes!

L.D. We ain't playin' no dominoes tonight, Colonel.

COLONEL. Why not?

L.D. 'Cause tonight we're gonna have us a real meetin'!

RED. What the hell you talkin' about?

L.D. Tonight we're gonna have us a real live initiation.

SKIP. You mean to tell us that somebody wants to join the lodge?

L.D. That's right.

RED. Well, ah'll be damned.

L.D. Brother Knight Rufe Phelps here has got us a new man, ain't you, Brother Knight Phelps?

RUFE. (*Grinning and Shuffling.*) Yes, sir, ah have.

OLIN. You never told me 'bout no new man whilst we was a-playin' horseshoes.

RUFE. Ah was gonna, till you started cheatin'.

OLIN. Ah never cheated! You're the one that cheats. Any time you throw one four feet from the stake you call it a dadburned leaner!

L.D. All right now, damnit, let's git on with it! Brother Knight Phelps, tell us 'bout our new brother-to-be.

RUFE. Ah got us Lonnie Roy McNeil. He's old Grady McNeil's boy from over there in Silver City . . .

COLONEL. *Silver City!* Ah won't have him!

RUFE. (*Taken aback.*) He's a real nice feller, Colonel.

COLONEL. Don't give a damn; if he's from Silver City he's no damn good!

SKIP. Well, hell, Colonel, it's not like he's from the Congo or somethin'. My God, Silver City's only three miles away.

L.D. Ah think it's a right good idea that we branch out a little, Colonel. Ah mean, nobody from Bradleyville has joined the lodge for over five years now.

COLONEL. People from Silver City are low-down stinkin' cowards and ah flat will not have them around!

RUFE. Well, hell, ah didn't know *Silver City* was on our list too!

L.D. Now, Colonel, you know we all respect your judgment in ever'thang but . . .

COLONEL. You damn well better.

L.D. But maybe we would all understand a little better if we all knew *why* people from Silver City was no damn good.

COLONEL. Because in nineteen hundred and eighteen Staff Sergeant George Plummer from right over yonder in Silver City refused to fight, that's why! Whey-faced little coward jest stood there in the trench with his puttees floppin' around and puke all over his face, hands shakin' and spit runnin' out his mouth. Kept mumblin' over and over, "Who am ah? Who am ah?" Well, ah knew damn well who he was, he was Staff Sergeant George Plummer from over there to *Silver City.* Ah ordered that little son-of-a-bitch to climb up . . . people from Silver City are no damn good. That is an order and that is a fact.

L.D. Well, hell, Colonel, this-here feller wantin' to join ain't no Plummer, he's a McNeil.

RUFE. That's right, Colonel, he's old Grady McNeil's boy.

COLONEL. He's from *Silver City*, ain't he?

RUFE. Well, yes, but . . .

COLONEL. Well, there you are.

L.D. Well, actually, he ain't exactly from Silver City, Colonel. Ah mean, not from right there smack in the town. The McNeil place is sorter outside the town, isn't it, Rufe?

RUFE. Well, yeah, kindly out on the rural route there.

COLONEL. Not in the town, huh?

RUFE. No, sir. Now, Lonnie Roy works there in Silver City but he lives sorter out, you know.

COLONEL. Well, ah don't know. You're sure now he's not a Plummer?

RUFE. Oh no, sir, Colonel, he's a McNeil, okay and he's shore wantin' to be a Lodge brother. Ah talked to him day affore yesterday over to the Silver City Pipe Fittin' Company and he said he would come over here tonight for shore.

COLONEL. Which McNeil is that?

L.D. Grady McNeil's boy, Colonel. From over there to Silver, uh, uh, from over yonder.

COLONEL. That the Grady McNeil that married the oldest Richey girl?

RUFE. No, ah think Lonnie Roy's Mama was a Spencer, weren't she, Olin?

OLIN. (*Who is an expert in these matters, therefore he pronounces each name very distinctly.*) She was *Maude Spencer* affore she married *Grady McNeil* over there to, uh, by Silver City. I know this 'cause a bunch of my cousins is *Spencers* and *Maude* was the second-oldest girl next to *Winifred Spencer*, who married a P & G soap salesman from Amarillo.

RUFE. By God, that's right. I remember that. Married him kindly on the sly, didn't she?

OLIN. They e-loped up to Durant, Oklahoma. Made her pa mad as hell. He didn't want *Winifred* married to no drummer. Ah remember 'cause her brother *Clete* an' me was pullin' a water well once out to the *Honeycutt* place and . . .

RED. For Christ's sake, let's git on with the meetin'!

OLIN. Ah jest thought you-all wanted to know.

RED. Well, we don't. Come on, L.D., let's git on with it.

L.D. Yes, well, it sounds like Lonnie Roy's got himself a real fine background, Brother Knight Potts.

OLIN. (*Smugly.*) Figgered you-all wanted to know.

RUFE. That the same Clete Spencer that drowned out to Lake Bradleyville?

SKIP. For Christ's sake!

OLIN. No, if you recall, there was two *Clete Spencers*. You see *Winifred's* daddy married twice. Now the *Clete Spencer* ah was pullin' the well with was known as *"Big Clete"* Spencer 'cause he was borned to old man *Spencer's* first wife, *Bessie*, who was also the mama of *Winifred* and *Maude*, but the other *Clete Spencer*, who was knowed as *"Little Clete"* and who drowned out to Lake Bradleyville, was borned to old man *Spencer's* second wife, *Mary*, who was also the mama of . . .

SKIP. Jesus Christ. Sure, Olin, we all know the story. Now come on, let's git on with the meetin'.

RUFE. You don't want to git on with the meetin'. You jest want to git on with the refreshments.

SKIP. Ah do not!

RED. The hell you don't. Your tongue's hangin' out so far now it looks like a necktie.

COLONEL. Onward, onward. Quit dilly-dallyin' around. Git the job done. The A.E.F. never wasted time. Never would have whipped the Hun if we had. Git the job done.

L.D. Yes, sir, Colonel. Now, as ah was sayin' . . . (*He is interrupted by a commotion outside the door. Shouts and bangs.*)

OLIN. (*Leaping up.*) Oh, my God, what's that?

(*The door bursts open and* Ramsey-Eyes *appears, securely holding on to a young man*—Lonnie Roy McNeil.)

RAMSEY-EYES. Ah got him! Ah got him! He was tryin' to sneak into the meetin', Mistah L.D., sah, but ah glommed onto him affore he could.

LONNIE. Tell this crazy fool to turn me loose!

RUFE. Let him go, Ramsey-Eyes, this here is Lonnie Roy McNeil.

RAMSEY-EYES. (*Releasing him.*) You mean he belongs up here?

RED. That's right, *he* belongs up here, but *you* don't. Now git your butt back down to the lobby where it does belong.

RAMSEY-EYES. Yes, sah, ah only wishes you-all would tell me who am a Magnolia and who ain't, thass all. (*Exits.*)

COLONEL. What happened, what's goin' on?

L.D. Nuthin', Colonel Kinkaid. Jest a little misunderstandin', that's all.

SKIP. Ramsey-Eyes jest made a little mistake, Colonel, that's all.

COLONEL. Ramsey-Eyes. He a member now?

L.D. 'Course he ain't no member, Colonel, he jest caught somebody outside, thinkin' it was an in-truder.

COLONEL. Caught him a spy, did he? Good man, that Ramsey-Eyes. Good soldier.

RUFE. Only it weren't no spy. It was Lonnie Roy McNeil, our new member.

RED. Stupid black, dumb butt!

(*They all turn and contemplate* Lonnie Roy. *He is a thin, big-eyed kid in an ill-fitting suit, his hair is bowl cut and he wears tennis shoes. Born on a little farm just outside Silver City, Texas,* Lonnie Roy *had watched his older brothers march off to Korea and envisioned a military career for himself. However, physical defects, asthma, and flat feet kept him out of service. He left high school in his sophomore year and was employed by a pipe-fitting concern. For a while he enjoyed the company of his fellow dropouts and high-school chums—driving around in pickup trucks, smoking cigarettes, and drinking beer—but soon the long arm of the draft board and in one or two cases, the state penitentiary in Huntsville cut his peer group down to one.* Lonnie Roy *found himself enjoying the comradeship of absolutely no one at all until one day* Rufe Phelps *dropped into Silver City to buy some pipe.*)

L.D. Howdy there, Lonnie Roy. Mah name is L. D. Alexander and ah wish to welcome you to the Knights of the White Magnolia.

LONNIE. Jeeezus, that's one mean man you got out there.

L.D. Ah hell, boy, Ramsey-Eyes ain't one of us. He jest sweeps up the place, that's all.

LONNIE. Oh well, ah guess that's all right then. You sure now he ain't . . .

L.D. Hell no! Now come on and meet the fellow knights. This here is Red Grover.

RED. How are you?

L.D. Rufe Phelps you already know. (*They nod.*) Olin Potts over by the door there.

OLIN. Your mama is *Maude Spencer McNeil*, ain't she?

LONNIE. Yes, sir, she is.

OLIN. Knew it!

L.D. Skip Hampton.

SKIP. Howdy.

L.D. And Colonel J. C. Kinkaid.

COLONEL. Retired. Glad to know you, Lonnie Roy. What branch you serve in?

LONNIE. Beg pardon.

COLONEL. Army, Navy, Marines, Army Air Corps?

LONNIE. Oh, that. Nuthin'.

COLONEL. Nuthin'?

LONNIE. I git the asthma sometimes.

COLONEL. Well, what the hell.

LONNIE. (*Lifting a tennis-shoe-clad foot.*) An mah feet is flat.

COLONEL. Jesus Christ!

LONNIE. Well, gawlee, ah cain't help it.

L.D. The Colonel here was in the A.E.F.

LONNIE. The what?

L.D. The American Army in World's War I.

LONNIE. Ah don't reckon ah ever studied much on them ancient wars and such like.

COLONEL. Blackball the flat-footed asthmatic, *Silver City* son-of-a-bitch!

LONNIE. Hell, ah never meant nuthin'.

L.D. 'Course you didn't, Lonnie Roy. The Colonel here is jest a little crusty, that's all. He don't mean no harm.

RED. Jest an old war horse, right, Colonel?

COLONEL. Better an old war horse than a young jackass!

L.D. Now, you jest sit down right here, Lonnie Roy, and we'll git on with the meetin'. Then afterwards we'll all have us a little nip. How's that sound?

SKIP. Sounds damn good to me.

L.D. Shut up, Skip.

LONNIE. Fine, fine. A little nip would go down real good.

SKIP. Sure would!

RED. Shut up, Skip!

L.D. Now, Lonnie Roy, affore ah ad-minister the oath of membership, ah want to tell you a little bit about the Knights of the White Magnolia.

LONNIE. Rufe already told me about the domino games. Sounds real good to me.

RUFE. Old Lonnie Roy here really likes them dominoes.

LONNIE. You bet! Moon, Forty-two, ah like to play 'em all.

OLIN. We play mostly Forty-two here, Lonnie Roy.

LONNIE. And when he told me that this-here lodge was for white men only, well, sir, ah was sold. Sold right there on the spot.

L.D. That's fine, Lonnie Roy, but now let me tell you about the rest . . .

LONNIE. When Rufe come over to the pipe-fittin' company and told me about this-here lodge, ah said right off, "Sign me up," didn't ah, Rufe?

RUFE. Shore did. Ah was over there buyin' some pipe for mah cesspool . . .

31

LONNIE. You can git it over yonder a whole lot cheaper than here in Bradleyville.

RUFE. That's the damn truth.

L.D. Well, that's fine, now . . .

OLIN. What you gittin' for pipe over there, Lonnie Roy?

L.D. Damnit to hell, now you all shut up and let me finish.

OLIN. Well, all ah wanted to know was . . .

RED. Shut up, Olin!

COLONEL. What's happenin'? What's goin' on?

SKIP. Red won't let L.D. git on with the meetin'.

RED. The hell you say! Ah never done nuthin'. It was Olin.

OLIN. Ah never done nuthin'.

COLONEL. Shut the hell up, all of you! Now damnit, L.D., git on with the meetin'. By gawd, ah wish ah'd had the bunch of you over there in France. You'd have shaped up then, by Gawd.

L.D. Yes, sir, Colonel . . . now . . .

COLONEL You'd have shaped up or ah'da kicked some butts!

L.D. Yes, sir, Colonel.

COLONEL. No goddamned gabbin' around in the trenches. Find yourself strung out on the wire like a piece of pork. Piece of pork.

L.D. Please, Colonel. If ah can continue.

COLONEL. Yes, yes, continue. Who the hell's stoppin' you?

L.D. Nobody, Colonel, it's jest that . . .

COLONEL. You let me know who's stoppin' you, L.D., and ah'll put him up again' the by-God wall.

SKIP. Goddamnit, Colonel Kinkaid, shut up!

(There is a long, stunned silence. All turn and look at Skip.)

COLONEL. Who said that! (Silence.) Who said that, as said!!!

SKIP. (Meekly.) Ah did, Colonel.

COLONEL. You know the last person who ever dared say that to me?

SKIP. No, sir.

COLONEL. (Animated and cheery.) General Pershing, that's who. Old Black Jack himself. (Chuckles.) We was down in Mexico at the time and ah was a snotnosed shavetail. Well, sir, one afternoon at the officers' mess . . .

L.D. Please, Colonel, let's save the story till refreshment time, okay?

RED. Shore, Colonel, let's hold her off till then.

COLONEL. Sure, sure, sure. (Chuckles.) Old Black Jack himself.

L.D. Now, Lonnie Roy, as ah was sayin', bein' a member of the Knights of the White Magnolia is actual bein' a member of a brotherhood. Ah

32

mean, you can look on any of us fellers here just like we was your own brothers, your own blood kin.

LONNIE. (*Sincerely.*) That there's real nice to know.

L.D. The Knights of the White Magnolia was founded back in 1902, when Knight Brother Maynard C. Stempco of Austin got fed up to his ears with the way the Ku Klux was runnin' things and broke off to form his own outfit. Well, sir, the idea growed and growed and by the late 1920's there was Knights of the White Magnolia lodges all over Texas and parts of Oklahoma.

LONNIE. My gosh. How's come Mr. Stempco got fed up with the Klan?

RED. 'Cause anybody that's got to put on a white bedsheet to kick a coon's ass has got to be a damn fool, that's why

LONNIE. Oh, yeah, sure, I see.

L.D. Why in 1939 we had us a con-vention in Tulsa, Oklahoma, that was attended by two thousand people.

RUFE. The Colonel was there. Weren't you, Colonel?

COLONEL. Got drunk and threw up all over my wheelchair. Made the wheels sticky.

LONNIE. You still have them con-ventions?

L.D. Well, uh, no, not in a long time, but we're workin' on it, ain't we, Red?

RED. (*Amused.*) Oh hell, yes.

LONNIE. Well, how's come you don't have 'em regular?

L.D. Stupidity, Lonnie Roy. Pure by-God dumb stupidity. People got to where they didn't want to join up any more. Can you imagine that? They didn't want to he Knights of the White Magnolia. They wanted to be Jaycees or Toast Masters or Elks or Lions or Moose, they wanted to be by-God animals, that's right, animals, but not knights. They turned around and stabbed their granddaddies square in the back. Turned up their noses on their race, started kowtowin' to all them-there mi-norities, and little by little the lodges jest sorter dried up. Nobody wanted to join. No new people. Jesus, but we was big once, Lonnie Roy. Hell, there was governors and senators that was Brother Knights. We had con-ventions and barbecues and parades. Took over a whole hotel there in Tulsa. Gawd, and it musta been somethin' to see. Bands playin' and baton girls a-marchin'along. The Grand Imperial Wizard of the brotherhood rode in a big open carriage pulled by six white horses, and up above the whole shebang was this great old big blimb towin' this-here banner sayin' TULSA WELCOMES THE KNIGHTS OF THE WHITE MAG-NOLIA. Gawda mighty, now wasn't that somethin'!

LONNIE. Jeezus, you mean to say that with all that great stuff, that people quit joinin' up?

L.D. That's right, Lonnie Roy.

LONNIE. My God, why?

L.D. Ah don't know, Lonnie Roy, ah honestly don't know. When Red an' me come into the lodge after World's War II, why there musta been fifteen or twenty members. Then fellers jest started a-droppin' out—quit comin'. Oh, ever' now and then somebody would join up, like Skip here, he joined up after Ko-rea.

LONNIE. You was in Ko-rea?

SKIP. Damn right. Blastin' them gooks. Ah was hell on wheels with a B.A.R. Regular John Wayne. Right, Red?

RED. That's what you keep tellin' ever'body.

SKIP. Ah'll never forget the time me an' Dale Laverty was bringin' them Marines down from that-there Chosan reservoir.

RED. For Christ's sake, shut up! We heard that damn story a hundred times.

SKIP. (*To Lonnie.*) Ah'll tell you all about it after the meetin', okay?

LONNIE. Swell.

SKIP. It's a hell of a good story.

RUFE. Me and Olin have been members since nineteen and forty-eight, ain't we, Olin?

OLIN. January 24th, 1948. Damn right.

LONNIE. You mean, you fellers is all the members there is?

RUFE. Well, there's Milo Crawford, but he had to take his mama over to Big Spring.

RED. Him and his damn mama. Makes you puke.

LONNIE. What about all the lodges in the other towns?

L.D. There ain't any more.

LONNIE. You mean they're all gone?

L.D. Ever' one of em.

RED. We're what you might call the last of the Mo-hicans, boy.

LONNIE. But how can you-all keep this-here room for your meetin's, don't it cost a lot of money?

L.D. Nope. You see the Colonel there owns the hotel.

LONNIE. Oh, ah see.

RED. Don't pay no dues to this club, boy. Jest lots of fun and lots of whiskey.

L.D. But the most important thing is the fact that you're wantin' to join up.

LONNIE. Me? Ah'm important?

L.D. Shore you are. You see, you can git other smart young fellers like yourself interested in the lodge.

RUFE. Damn right. You may be the start of a whole new movement, boy.

LONNIE. Well, ah don't know many fellers mah age over to home. Most of 'em are either gone off somewhere or are in the army.

L.D. But you are a start, don't you see? Yes, sir, a start. Hell, we may be beginnin' a whole new ball game here.

LONNIE. Ah could maybe talk to some of the fellers at the pipe company.

L.D. There you go!

LONNIE. (*Getting excited.*) And mah daddy knows lots and lots of folks.

L.D. Damn right! Now you're talkin', boy!

RUFE. By gollies, L.D., maybe we got somethin' here. Maybe we can catch on again.

L.D. Shore we can. Anythin' can happen. Hell's fire, stuff like this has happened affore. Outfits git kindly down like and jest one little thang gits 'em goin' again, and wham, next thang you know they're back on the top. Bigger and better than affore.

OLIN. You mean big like we was in nineteen and thirty-nine?

L.D. Sure, why not? Bigger!

SKIP. Oh, for Christ's sake!!!

L.D. What the hell's wrong with you?

SKIP. You guys are crazy. Jesus Christ, we git one new member in five years and ten minutes later we're bigger than the by-God Woodman of the World.

OLIN. It don't do no harm to plan.

SKIP. Plan! This ain't no plan, it's a dream—a damn-fool dream.

L.D. You tryin' to say we're damn fools!

SKIP. No, no, ah ain't sayin that. It's only . . .

RED. Only what? If you don't like bein' a member of this goddamn brotherhood, why the hell don't you say so?

SKIP. Ah didn't say that, all ah said was . . .

COLONEL. What's goin' on?

RUFE. Skip Hampton says he don't want to be a knight no more.

SKIP. No, ah never. All as said was . . .

COLONEL Shoot the goddamned desertin' son-of-a-bitch!

SKIP. Ah ain't desertin'! All ah said was . . .

COLONEL. Shoot 'em! By God, we shot 'em in France. No reason why we can't shoot 'em right here in Bradleyville.

OLIN. Actual, Skip can't help bein' the way he is, what with his grand-mother on his daddy's side bein' a *Bentley.*

COLONEL. A Bentley!

SKIP. Oh, my God!

OLIN. All them Bentleys was mean. Now ah don't want to give no disre-spect to your kinfolk there, Skip, but if you'll look back a bit you'll see jest how mean them *Bentleys* was.

SKIP. Who gives a damn!

OLIN. You ought to! Ah mean, if ah had *Bentley* blood in me, ah damn shore would give a damn.

SKIP. Well, ah don't!

OLIN. Well, you ought to!

RUFE. You better listen to Olin there, Skip. When it comes to kinfolk, old Olin there knows what he's talkin' about.

SKIP. Well, why the hell don't we talk about somethin' else! Jesus, ah'm sick and tired of listenin' to whose Uncle Abraham is married to which Cousin Clarabelle's cross-eyed stepsister.

RUFE. You're jest jealous 'cause Olin here can remember all them names and you cain't remember nuthin'.

SKIP. So he can remember names. So damn what! Let's make him the by-God county clerk and fire the bookkeeper. He can sit on his butt and babble Abernathy to Zackafoozass all day long.

OLIN. Well, now that ain't a very nice thang to say.

RED. Yeah, Skip, why the hell don't you shut up.

SKIP. Shut up, yourself, damnit! Where the hell you git off tellin' people to shut up!

RED. You'd better watch your step there, sonny boy!

L.D. Now, now, Brothers, let's jest all stand back and cool off a spell. Remember, we got us a new member here. We don't want him to git no wrong ideas about us now, do we?

COLONEL. Shoot him!

LONNIE. My gosh. Do you fellers fight like this all the time?

RED. Only on meetin' nights.

LONNIE. Maybe ah'd better go home and come back next time.

L.D. No need of that. We're jest horsin' around, that's all. Havin' lots of fun is part of bein' a brother. Why, the best part of the meetin' is comin' up, the initiation, and after that the refreshments. You don' wanna miss that, do you?

LONNIE. No, ah jest thought . . .

L.D. Well, hell no, you don't! We gotta initiation for you, Lonnie Roy McNeil, that's gonna be the high by-God point of your life.

LONNIE. You ain't gonna hit me with paddles and such like, are you?

L.D. Hell no! That there's kid stuff, this-here initiation is based on God and brotherhood.

RUFE. It's a hell of an impressive sight, Lonnie Roy—you see, we light up the cross and . . .

OLIN. No fair tellin'! We ain't started yet.

RUFE. Well, hell, ah didn't *tell* nuthin', all ah said was . . .

COLONEL. Let's git on with it! Good God, you men shilly-shally and fart around worse than the Fifth Marines!

SKIP. Hell yes, let's git started!

L.D. All right, damnit, we will!

COLONEL. Bumble-dickin' around. That's all you fellers do.

L.D. Yes, well, all right, Colonel. We will now commence with the ceremony of initiation.

OLIN. Wait a minute. We can't start no ceremony yet.

L.D. Why the hell not?

OLIN. 'Cause we ain't voted on him yet.

SKIP. Oh, for Christ's sake.

OLIN. We gotta vote! Them there's the rules.

SKIP. We didn't have no goddamn vote when I got initiated.

RED. It's a damn-good thing for you that we didn't.

SKIP. What the hell's that spozed to mean?

RED. Jest what I said, that's what.

L.D. All right now, that's jest a by-God nuff! Ah want it quiet in here and ah mean dead quiet. (*Silence.*) That's a whole lot better. All right now, Olin, if you insist, we will . . .

COLONEL. Bumble-dick, bumble-dick, bumble-dick.

L.D. (*Patiently.*) Yes, Colonel, that's right. Now . . .

COLONEL. That's what old Black Jack did. Bumble-dicked all over Mexico. Let that fat little greaser Pancho Villa make a damn fool of him. Betcha didn't know that, did you?

L.D. No, Colonel, we didn't. Now . . .

COLONEL. Well, he did.

L.D. Please, Colonel, we gotta git on with the vote.

COLONEL. What we votin' on?

L.D. On Lonnie Roy, Colonel.

COLONEL. Who?

L.D. Lonnie Roy McNeil, our new member.

COLONEL. We got a new member? Well, it's about time; who is it?

RUFE. Lonnie Roy McNeil, Colonel, Grady McNeil's boy from over there to Silver . . . from over yonder.

COLONEL. Well, ah'll be damned. You don't bumble-dick around, do you, young feller?

LONNIE. No, sir!

COLONEL. That's good. The Germans will get you if you do.

LONNIE. (*With deep conviction.*) Well, ah never do.

COLONEL. Come over the top and stick one of them spiky helmets right up your butt.

SKIP. Jesus H. God Almighty, that's the damnedest thang ah ever heard of in my life.

COLONEL. What the hell's wrong with you?

SKIP. Them Germans ain't wore no spiky helmets in fifty years.

COLONEL. Don't mean they ain't gonna put them on again! You-all think the Kaiser's dead, don't you? Well, he ain't! Him and Crown Prince Willie is both livin' on a cattle ranch in Argentina and in secret is storin' up guns in the basements of Catholic churches all over the world.

SKIP. That ain't no Kaiser that's down there in Argentina. That there's *Hitler!* Hell, we've had a whole new world's war since the damn Kaiser was runnin' around.

LONNIE. That's right. Ah remember readin' about old Hitler in school. Why, he was on the German side in World's War II.

RUFE. Only he ain't in Argentina, no, sir. Ah read in a magazine over to Billberry's Drugstore how them Russians got old Hitler hid out in a little room over there in Mos-cow.

LONNIE. No kiddin'.

RUFE. Sure. They smuggled him out of Berlin in a hay wagon.

COLONEL. Skinny little son-of-a-bitch couldn't hold a candle to the Kaiser.

RED. Good God! We gonna git on with the votin' or not?

L.D. Damn right! Now, everybody in this-here membership wantin' Lonnie Roy McNeil to be a brother knight, put up their hand.

OLIN. Hold it.

L.D. Now what?

OLIN. Lonnie Roy here has got to be out of the room when we make this-here vote. That there's a rule. Ain't it, Rufe?

RUFE. Ah recollect on how it is.

L.D. Oh, what the hell. Lonnie Roy, would you please leave the room while we have our vote here.

LONNIE. Shore.

L.D. Won't take a second. We'll be callin' you right back.

LONNIE. (*Moving toward the door.*) That's okay, ah'll jest wait outside.

RUFE. Nuthin' to worry about, Lonnie Roy. We jest gotta follow the rules, you know.

LONNIE. Sure, that's okay.

OLIN. Rules is rules.

LONNIE. Fine. (*He exits.*)

L.D. Okay now, ever'body sit down and we'll com-mence with the votin' Not you, Olin!

OLIN. How come not me?

L.D. 'Cause you are the door guard tonight.

OLIN. The door guard?

L.D. You gotta stand up there and guard the door while we have our vote and initiation so's nobody that ain't a Magnolia will slip in on us durin' the ceremony.

OLIN. Well, ah don't wanna stand up all the time.

L.D. Well, you gotta.

OLIN. Why cain't I sit down and put my foot up agin' the door?

L.D. 'Cause you cain't, that's why.

COLONEL. You are the sentry, Olin, and sentries don't sit, they stand and they stand tall.

OLIN. (*Grumbling.*) Yes, sir.

RED. (*Chuckling.*) Rules is rules, Olin.

OLIN. (*Mimicking Red's voice.*) Rules is rules, Olin.

L.D. We will now have our vote.

COLONEL. What we votin' on?

L.D. On Lonnie Roy, Colonel.

COLONEL. Am ah for him or agin him?

L.D. You're for him, Colonel.

COLONEL. Hell, ah thought ah was agin him.

(*There is another loud commotion outside and* Milo Crawford *bursts through the door with* Lonnie Roy *in tow. Milo is mild-mannered, lank, gangly, and very homely. He wears a white shirt, a dark necktie, and an old double-breasted brown suit.*)

RUFE. Milo Crawford.

OLIN. Milo.

MILO. Looky here, looky here. Ah caught this-here feller sneakin' around outside the door!

L.D. Let him go, Milo, this here is Lonnie Roy McNeil. He's a new member.

MILO. A new member?

L.D. Yes, damnit, a new member!

MILO. Well, gosh, ah didn't know.

RED. Well, you know now, you damned fool! So turn him loose!

MILO. (*Releasing him.*) Shucks ah'm plumb sorry, feller. Ah didn't know.

LONNIE. That's okay.

COLONEL. What's goin' on?

L.D. Nuthin', Colonel.

MILO. Shucks, Colonel, ah didn't know.

COLONEL. Who are you?

MILO. Milo Crawford, Colonel.

COLONEL. Ah thought you took your mama to Big Spring.

MILO. Couldn't get mah danged old pickup started.

OLIN. You try pumpin' her?

MILO. Yeah, but it didn't do no good. Ah jest don't seem to git no gas.

RUFE. Probable the fuel line.

MILO. Speck so.

OLIN. Or the carburetor . . .

L.D. Well, anyway, since you're here now, go on over there and shake hands with Lonnie Roy McNeil.

MILO. (*Shaking hands.*) Pleased to meet you. How's come ah never seed you around affore? You new in town or somethin'?

LONNIE. No, sir. Ah live over to Silver City.

COLONEL. Silver City!

RUFE. (*Covering up.*) He's a helluva nice guy. Milo.

OLIN. He's old Grady McNeil's boy, Milo.

MILO. I see.

L.D. Well, now that we all know each other, let's please, please, git on with the votin'.

MILO. What we votin' on?

L.D. We're votin' on Lonnie Roy here.

COLONEL. Who?

RED. *Lonnie Roy McNeil!!*

COLONEL. Ah thought we already done that .

SKIP. We was, but Milo Crawford messed ever'thang up.

COLONEL. Milo Crawford? Ah thought he went over to Big Spring.

MILO. Ah couldn't get mah pickup started, Colonel.

40

COLONEL. You try pushin' her?

RUFE. Won't do no good to push her if she ain't gittin' any gas.

OLIN. Probable the carburetor.

MILO. Speck so.

RED. (*Sarcastically.*) What happened to Mama, Milo? She gotta stay home all by herself tonight?

MILO. No. George and Jane Williams come by and give her a ride.

RED. Ooo-eee, ain't that nice!

SKIP. Let's git on with the votin'!

RUFE. Hell, yes. Let's git on with it.

L.D. Okay, Okay. Lonnie Roy, would you please ... (*He indicates the door.*)

LONNIE. Shore thing. (*He goes out.*)

MILO. Where's he goin'?

L.D. Outside.

MILO. Why?

L.D. Rules.

MILO. Rules?

L.D., RED, OLIN, SKIP, AND RUFE. Rules!!!

MILO. I see.

L.D. Okay. Ever'body wantin' Lonnie Roy McNeil for a new member, put up their hand. (*They all do except the* Colonel.) What's wrong, Colonel, why ain't you votin'?

COLONEL. Votin'? What for?

L.D. Go over and put up the Colonel's hand, will you, Red.

RED. Shore thing. (*He does.*)

COLONEL. What's goin' on? What's goin' on?

L.D. Nuthin', Colonel. Red's jest helpin' you to vote, that's all.

COLONEL. Oh, well, thank you, Red. Damn nice of you.

RED. Mah pleasure, Colonel.

L.D. Fine, fine. That's real official-like. Okay, Brother Knight Potts, you can bring in Lonnie Roy now.

OLIN. Okay. (*He opens the door.*) All right, Lonnie Roy, you-all can come in now. Lonnie Roy? Lonnie Roy? (*He steps outside.*) Well, what the hell!

L.D. What's wrong?

OLIN. (*Sticking his head back into the room.*) He's gone.

(*They all freeze in place as the lights fade to blackout.*)

ACT II

The scene opens in the meeting room seconds later. The characters are found in positions held at the end of Act I. As the lights come up, they remain frozen for a moment before the dialogue begins.

L.D. What the hell you mean, he's gone?

OLIN. He's gone, he ain't out here.

L.D. Well, damnit, go look for him. See if Ramsey-Eyes saw where he went.

OLIN. Okay. (*He exits.*)

RED. Well, whattayou know about that.

L.D. He'll be back, he didn't have no reason to run off or anythin'.

COLONEL. What's happened? What's goin' on?

SKIP. Lonnie Roy's gone, Colonel.

COLONEL. Gone? Gone where?

SKIP. We don't know, Colonel.

L.D. He ain't gone, ah tell you.

RED. What kinda fellers you bringin' around here, Rufe? Runnin' away from an initiation.

RUFE. Well, hell, Red, ah don't know. He seemed like a nice-enough feller to me.

MILO. Ah didn't like the looks of him the first time ah laid eyes on him.

COLONEL. Shoot the son-of-a-bitch!

(*There is a knock at the door.*)

L.D. Ah'll bet that's him now. You see, ah told you he never run off. Come in, Brother Elect Knight of the White Magnolia, *Lonnie Roy McNeil!*

(*The door opens and* Ramsey-Eyes *comes in.*)

RAMSEY-EYES. 'Scuse me.

RED. What the hell you doin' up here!

RAMSEY-EYES. (*Feisty.*) Mistah Olin Potts done told me to come up hyare and tell you iffen ah seed where Mistah Lonnie Roy McNeil went to!

L.D. Well, did you?

RAMSEY-EYES. No, sah, but he never went out through de lobby 'cause ah been sittin' down dere by de door.

RUFE. Where's Olin now?

RAMSEY-EYES. He's gone over to see iffen Mistah Lonnie Roy McNeil went down and out de back way.

L.D. Did the clerk see anythin'?

RAMSEY-EYES. No, sah, he didn't see nuthin' 'cause he's been asleep for 'most an hour. But not me, no, sah, ah been wide awake all evenin'.

COLONEL. Good man, Ramsey-Eyes.

RAMSEY-EYES. Ah been keepin' guard, Colonel Kinkaid, sah.

COLONEL. Damn good man.

RAMSEY-EYES. Thank you, sah.

COLONEL. Back on down to your post now, Ramsey-Eyes.

RAMSEY-EYES. Thank you, sah. Yes, sah. (*Exiting.*) Ah been wide awake all evenin'.

RED. (*Muttering.*) Stupid idiot wouldn't recognize Lonnie Roy if he fell over him.

COLONEL. Faithful employee, that Ramsey-Eyes.

L.D. Sure, Colonel, sure.

COLONEL. Ah would trust that man with anythin' ah owned. (*To Rufe.*) General Pershing once commanded Neegrow troops, betcha didn't know that, did you?

RUFE. (*Interested.*) No, Colonel, I didn't.

COLONEL. Montana territory, October 1895. Troop of the 10th Cavalry. Neegrow troops. "Buffalo soldiers," the Injuns called 'em.

RUFE. Well, I'll be damned.

SKIP. Aw to hell with it, let's break open the booze.

RED. Gittin' a little shaky there, Skip?

SKIP. No, ah jest don't see any reason not to now.

RED. Whattayou think, L.D.?

L.D. I don't know. It jest don't figger. You know that kid seemed interested, really interested.

RED. Yeah, well, seein' as how our hope for the future done vanished into thin air, let's drink to the one who got away. (*He takes one of the bottles out of the bag.*) Who's first?

(*Skip reaches frantically for the bottle just as we hear a timid little knock at the door and* Lonnie Roy *sticks his head in the room.*)

LONNIE. Votin' all over with?

RED. Where the hell you been?

LONNIE. Ah hadda go pee.

SKIP. Jesus H. Christ on a crutch.

LONNIE. Well, ah hadda.

RED. Looks like we're gonna have an initiation after all, Skip.

SKIP. Aw, come on, Red, jest one shot, jest one.

RED. Sorry, Skip. Rules is rules.

LONNIE. Was ah voted in?

L.D. You sure was, Lonnie Roy. Ever'body voted for you. Ain't that somethin'?

LONNIE. Well. ah am truly gratified.

L.D. That jest shows you how much all the brothers think of you.

OLIN. (*Entering.*) Ah cain't find that stupid little son-of-a-bitch anywhere!

RUFE. He's here, Olin.

OLIN. Oh, yeah, well. Howdy there, Lonnie Roy.

LONNIE. Ah hadda go pee.

OLIN. Oh. Ah didn't think to look down the hall.

L.D. Well, ever'thin' is all right now. Now we can have our initiation.

SKIP. It's about by-God time.

L.D. (*Who has been looking behind the podium.*) Now wait just a minute here. Where's the book?

RED. What book?

L.D. The initiation book. It ain't on the shelf behind the speaker's thing here.

RED. Well, don't look at me. I ain't got it.

L.D. It's always been on this-here shelf, now it ain't. Now, who took it?

MILO. Ah ain't got it.

OLIN. Me neither.

L.D. Skip?

SKIP. Are you kidding!

L.D. Rufe?

RUFE. No, sir.

SKIP. What about the Colonel?

COLONEL. Who? What? What's goin' on?

L.D. We're tryin' to find the initiation book, Colonel.

COLONEL. Well, go ahead and find it! Who the hell's stoppin' you?

L.D. We was wonderin' if you had it, Colonel.

COLONEL. Had what?

RED. The goddamned initiation book!!!

COLONEL. Hell no, I ain't got no book!!

L.D. (*In a mild state of panic.*) Well—damn! How we gonna hold a ceremony without a book?

SKIP. Let's jest make one up.

L.D. What the hell you talkin' about?

SKIP. Make up our own ceremony. (*He stands in front of* Lonnie Roy.) Hokus-pokus Maynard C. Stempco, got ready, get set, Little Clete Spencer—zap! Lonnie Roy McNeil, you are now initiated. Let's have a drink.

MILO. That wouldn't be right. Lonnie Roy wouldn't be a proper member.

OLIN. No, sir, somethin' like that would be agin the rules.

SKIP. What rules?

RUFE. The rules of the order of the Knights of the White Magnolia, that's what rules!

SKIP. Well, hell, there ain't no Knights of the White Magnolia but us. So what difference does it make?

L.D. It makes plenty of difference. That rule book was writ by Maynard C. Stempco himself, way back in 1902. It's got secret valuable writin's in it.

RUFE. Damn right.

L.D. We gotta find that book.

RED. You sure it ain't back there on the shelf?

L.D. It ain't here, I tell you. Only thing on this damned shelf is a box of dominoes.

RUFE. Maybe it's in the room some place.

(*They all vaguely look around the room.*)

L.D. Well, look for it!

OLIN. Don't see it.

L.D. Hell, it ain't in here either. Now hold on just a second, let's jest hold on and think a little bit. Now, who the hell was the last man we initiated?

OLIN. Milo Crawford.

L.D. Milo, when was you initiated?

MILO. What year is this?

L.D. It's still 1962.

SKIP. It's been that way ever since January, Milo.

MILO. In nineteen hundred and fifty-seven.

L.D. You shore?

MILO. Yep. 'cause that's the year my mama had her nervous breakdown.

L.D. Yeah, well, who did the book readin'?

MILO. You did.

L.D. Oh yeah, ah spoze ah did.

RED. (*Taunting.*) What'd you do with the book, L.D.?

COLONEL. What's goin' on?

SKIP. L.D. lost the initiation book, Colonel.

COLONEL. That was a damn-fool thing to do, L.D.

L.D. Ah never lost nuthin'.

RUFE. Well, hell, L.D., you had it last.

LONNIE. Does this mean ah ain't gonna git initiated after all?

L.D. Of course you're gonna git initiated. Soon as ah can think where ah put that damn-fool book.

RED. Where'd you put it after you used it last?

L.D. Ah thought ah put it on that shelf behind the speaker's outfit.

OLIN. Well, that jest messes up ever'thin'.

MILO. Shore does.

LONNIE. This mean ah ain't gonna git initiated after all?

SKIP. Hell, let's have us a little dring, maybe it'll help us remember.

RED. Ah thought you drank to forgit.

SKIP. Forgit? Shore, ah drink to forgit, an' ah got plenty to forgit too. You know, the Colonel here ain't the only one that's seen fightin'. Ah seen it too, plenty of it.

RED. Shore you have.

SKIP. Ah have, ah tell you! Plenty of it! Over there in Ko-rea ah was in every combat sector there was.

RED. You never was in shit! That buddy of yours that married your sister told me you guys never got closer to any front lines than fifty miles.

SKIP. That ain't true.

L.D. (*Who has been deep in thought.*) Wait a minute! Wait a minute! Ah remember now! Ah gave the book to the Colonel.

MILO. The Colonel?

L.D. That's right, he asked me for it and ah gave it to him.

(*They all turn and look at the Colonel.*)

COLONEL. (*After a moment, very quietly.*) Ramsey-Eyes has it.

L.D. What was that, Colonel?

COLONEL. (*Louder.*) Ramsey-Eyes has it!

L.D. What in the name of Christ is Ramsey-Eyes doin' with it?

COLONEL. He keeps it for me.

L.D. Well, if that ain't the damnedest thing ah ever heard of in my life. You mean to tell me that you gave the Knights of the White Magnolia secret book to Ramsey-Eyes!

RED. Jeezus Christ!

COLONEL. No, ah didn't give it to him. Ah told you-all, ah jest let him keep it.

L.D. What the hell for?

COLONEL. 'Cause ah was afraid ah would lose it. Mah memory's been givin' me some troubles lately and ah didn't want to lose it.

L.D. But why Ramsey-Eyes? Why not one of the brothers?

COLONEL. Because for one thing he is an old and faithful employee, and for another thing ah wouldn't trust any of you bumble-dicks with the rule book if it were writ on the side of an elephant!

RED. Well, ah'll be damned.

COLONEL. Probably.

L.D. (*Resigned.*) Olin, would you please go down to the lobby and ask Ramsey-Eyes for the book.

OLIN. Shore thing. (*He exits.*)

LONNIE. Does this mean ah'm gonna git initiated now?

L.D. Yes, damnit, yes! Now sit down over there and shut up!

LONNIE. (*Sitting.*) Ah never done nuthin.

COLONEL. Bumble-dicks.

MILO. Gawlee, ah cain't git over it. Ramsey-Eyes, with the rule book.

RUFE. You reckin he read it?

RED. Hell, no!

SKIP. How you know?

RED. 'Cause he's too damn dumb even to write his own name. Much less *read* anything.

RUFE. Well, at least we know where it is.

MILO. Yes, that's true. You know, even in the darkest moments you can always find a little good.

RUFE. (*Impressed.*) By God, that's damn truthful, Milo.

MILO. Thank you.

RUFE. You orter write that one down some place and send it in to a magazine or somethin'.

MILO. Think so?

RUFE. Hell, yes. Whattayou think, Red?

RED. Who gives a damn!

SKIP. Why don't you write it on the shithouse wall over to Red's place?

L.D. Shut up, Skip.

COLONEL. "Shut up, Kinkaid." that's what old Black Jack said when we was out there in Mexico. Hot as hell one day there in the officers' mess. Wind blowin' the tent sides back and forth. Flap, flap, flap . . .

OLIN. (*Entering.*) Well, here it is. He had it in an old seegar box in a closet.

L.D. (*Taking the book.*) That's the damnedest thing ah ever heard in my life.

RED. Crazy old fool.

L.D. Okay, boys, let's git at it. (*Walks to the podium and opens the book.*) Okay. Now, Red, you come up here and stand by me. Now, Milo, you stand by the station of the moon. Olin, you stand by the station of the sun, and, Rufe, you stand by the station of the west wind. Let's see now, what part can we give the Colonel?

COLONEL. Don't want no part. Ah don't feel good. Ah got me a headache.

OLIN. You want ah should go down and git you an aspirin, Colonel?

COLONEL. Don't want no part.

RED. Forgit him. Let's git on with it.

COLONEL. Ah was havin' me a cup of coffee with the Major when old Black Jack come in. Well, sir, as luck would have it, he come in jest as I was sayin' to the Major, "Ah don't think we're ever gonna catch that fat little greaser if we stay out here in this damn Meheeko for five hundred years . . ." and the General he says to me he says . . . (*Voice trails off.*)

L.D. Lonnie Roy, you stand in front of Red and me.

LONNIE. Yes, sir.

L.D. Okay, Skip. You hand out the written parts.

SKIP. Right.

LONNIE. (*To Red.*) Boy, this is excitin', ain't it?

RED. (*Muttering.*) If you like hunred-year-old snatch, it's a gas.

(L.D. *takes some cards out of the book and hands them to* Skip. Skip *walks around handing out the written roles while* L.D. *takes the initiation hats out of the trunk. The hats are fez-type with ribbons on the back and emblems on the front. A half moon, a sunburst, a cloud with streamers for the west wind, a lamp for wisdom, a series of fountain-type lines for the truth, and a bolt of lightning for the wizard.*)

L.D. Now, Brothers, here are the *Chapeaux de rituale.* Milo, you are the moon. Olin, you are the sun. Rufe, you are the west wind. Skip, you are Wisdom the Guide to the Mystic Mountain.

SKIP. Hot damn.

L.D. Red, you are the Golden Fountain of Truth and ah am the Imperial Wizard.

(*The knights put on their hats and move back to their stations looking over their roles. As they are doing this, the* Colonel *says his lines.*)

COLONEL. Flap, flap, flap. Horses standin' round hip-shot, slappin' at flies with their tails, lots of flies buzzin' around.

OLIN. Hey, L.D., somethin's wrong with my hat.

L.D. Spin it around, Olin, you got it on backward.

RUFE. Hey, look at old Milo Crawford there.

(Milo's hat is much too big and is almost down over his ears.)

L.D. Milo, put that thing on the back of your head, you look like hell.

SKIP. Hey, Red, that thing you got on your head look a whole lot like somethin' ah got growin' on my butt.

RED. Go to hell!

L.D. Shut up, Skip!

RUFE. Ah cain't read my part.

L.D. Why the hell not?

RUFE. It's got a big splotch or somethin' right in the middle of it.

L.D. Well, read around the goddamn splotch!

RUFE. (Dubiously.) Okay.

L.D. Okay now, here we go. (He starts to read.) "You are now on a journey, initiate Lonnie Roy McNeil. A journey to seek the Golden Fountain of Truth that flows deep in the darkness of the Mystic Mountain."

LONNIE. Gawlee.

L.D. During your journey, initiate Lonnie Roy McNeil, you will converse with the great heavenly sages, and as you heed their advice, your reply will be "Stempco, Stempco, Stempco." Do you understand?

LONNIE. Stempco, Stempco, Stempco. Yes, sir.

L.D. But you are not alone, initiate Lonnie Roy McNeil. By your decision to become a Knight of the White Magnolia you have wisdom by your side to guide you toward truth.

SKIP. (Reading.) "Ah am wisdom. Ah am with you always as your friend and companion. Fear not as we begin our journey, for ah am here with you to place your footsteps on the right path toward truth."

LONNIE. Stempco, Stempco, Stempco.

L.D. Your first journey, initiate Lonnie Roy McNeil, is to the pale-blue grotto of the moon.

(Skip leads Lonnie Roy over to Milo.)

MILO. (Reading.) "Ah am the moon. By night ah cast beams down upon you, lightin' the way along your journey toward the truth."

LONNIE. Stempco, Stempco, Stempco.

L.D. You now travel, initiate Lonnie Roy McNeil, to the blazin' realm of the sun.

(Skip leads Lonnie Roy to Olin.)

OLIN. "Ah am the sun. Ah bring my warmin' rays and glorious beams to warm and comfort you durin' the day as you journey toward the truth."

LONNIE. Stempco, Stempco, Stempco.

L.D. You now travel, initiate Lonnie Roy McNeil, to the long low plains of the west wind.

(Skip *leads him to* Rufe.)

COLONEL. Flap, flap, flap . . .

RUFE. (*Reading with great difficulty.*) "Ah am the west w_____. Ah blow my balmy bree_____ er _____ the _____ren desert an_____ the sails of your craf_____ cross the sea of ignor_____ on your journey toward the truth. Hell, L.D., it don't make no sense readin' around this-here splotch.

L.D. It sounded jest fine, Rufe. Anyway, we got the idea.

COLONEL. Flap, flap, flap . . .

L.D. You now arrive, initiate Lonnie Roy McNeil, at the Mystic Mountain, wherein lies the Golden Fountain of Truth and the great white marble temple of the Imperial Wizard.

(Skip *brings* Lonnie Roy *to the podium and has him kneel down.*)

RED. (*Starting to read.*) "Ah am the Golden . . ." (*Just as he reads the* Colonel *says the role from memory.*)

COLONEL. "Ah am the Golden Fountain of Truth. I welcome travelers to my magic waters. Your journey has been long and hard, but rejoice now, pilgrim, your reward is at hand."

LONNIE. Stempco, Stempco, Stempco.

L.D. By God, Colonel, that was real fine. How was it, Red?

RED. (*Grinning.*) Letter-perfect.

L.D. Jesus, Colonel. You think you can remember the part of the Imperial Wizard too?

COLONEL. Shut your mouth, Lieutenant Kinkaid. You keep talkin' a lot of bull and I'll have you on the horseshit detail for the rest of the campaign.

RED. Offhand, L.D., ah'd say that wasn't it.

L.D. Yes, well, maybe ah'd better read it. "Ah am the Imperial Wizard. You have been guided by wisdom and aided by the sun, the moon, and the west wind to taste now the living waters of the Golden Fountain of Truth." Oh hell!

RED. What's wrong?

L.D. It says here that ah am now to give the initiate a drink of clear water from a silver cup. Ah forgot all about that.

OLIN. Ah could go down to the lobby for a Coke.

RED. How about a shot of booze?

MILO. That's what you gave me when ah was initiated.

RED. Did you take it?

MILO. Of course ah took it.

RED. Does your mama know about this?

MILO. Ah do lots of things my mama don't know about.

RED. Shore you do.

L.D. Okay, okay, let's do this right now. Give Lonnie Roy the bottle, Red.

RED. Okay. (*Opens the bottle, hands it to* Lonnie Roy.)

L.D. Let's see. Uh . . . Living waters of the Golden Fountain of Truth. Drink deeply, knight initiate Lonnie Roy McNeil, your quest has been rewarded.

(Lonnie Roy *takes a long pull.*)

RED. (*Grabbing the bottle.*) Not too damn deeply.

SKIP. How about a shot for his faithful companion?

L.D. Shut up, Skip. Now that you have known wisdom and tasted truth, knight initiate Lonnie Roy McNeil, you are ready to receive the final rites of membership. Light up the cross, Olin.

OLIN. Okay. (*He flips on the switch by the door. The cross comes on but the bulbs are so covered with dust, dirt, and fly specks that they are barely visible.*)

L.D. What's wrong with that damn thing?

OLIN. Sure seems dim-like.

RUFE. I'll jiggle it a little bit and maybe it'll come on better. (*He walks over to the cross and looks at it.*) Well, no damn wonder!

L.D. What's wrong?

RUFE. Well, it's all covered with dust and stuff.

L.D. Well, git somethin' and clean it off.

RUFE. Turn off the light, Olin. (*He pulls a chair over and stands on it to clean the bulbs with his handkerchief. Milo, Red, and Olin gather around to help him.*)

COLONEL. When General Pershing was a lieutenant, he was instructin' all them smarty-assed Kay-dets there at the West Point and they didn't like him. No, sir, they did not like him one little bit. So when they found out that he commanded them Nee-grow troops, they started callin' him Black Jack.

MILO. . . . Spit on the base affore you screw it back in.

RED. Somebody orter spit on your base.

COLONEL. But he fixed 'em. He jest held on to the name, you see. Made it famous, by God. Yes, sir, you can have your goddamn Ike's and Doug's, give me old Black Jack Pershing anytime. Yes, sir!

OLIN. Don't touch them wires there . . . they'll shock the hell outta you.

RUFE. How can they shock me? You got the switch turned off, ain't you?

OLIN. Shore I got it off, but don't you know electricity lingers.

51

RUFE. Electricity lingers . . . that's the dumbest thing I ever heard in mah life.

L.D. For Christ's sake, ain't you all finished yet?

RUFE. All done, L.D. Okay, Olin, you can fire it up again.

(Olin *does—the cross gleams more or less like new.*)

L.D. That's a lot better. Okay, Olin, you can turn off the room lights now.

(Olin *does. They all stand in the dim glow of the cross.*)

LONNIE. Gee, that's pretty.

OLIN. Ain't that somethin'!

MILO. It looks like church or somethin'. You know?

COLONEL. What's that glow up there? What is it?

L.D. We got the cross on, Colonel.

COLONEL. Used to fire them lights up in the sky over the trenches. Light things up real bright like, then commence to shootin'. Hated them damn lights.

RED. You and General Pershing, right, Colonel?

COLONEL. General Pershing? He told me to shut up one time. You know, he never said anythin' to me again, not one word, 'cept maybe to give an order or two. Ah don't think he liked me.

L.D. Shore, Colonel, shore. Now, Brother Knights, we come to the most important part of our initiation. This-here part ah'm about to read to you, Lonnie Roy McNeil, is the real meanin' of White Magnoliaism . . . (*The cross makes a few sputtering noises and goes out, pluging the room into darkness.*) What the hell? Turn on the lights, Olin.

OLIN. Ah'm gittin' there.

(*The lights go on.*)

L.D. Rufe, see if you can fix that damn thing.

Rufe. Hell, ah don't know what's wrong with it, L.D. It must have a short in it or somethin'.

L.D. Well, quit foolin' with it. We'll go on without it.

COLONEL. Don't like the goddamn dark!

RED. Git on with it, L.D. Ah'm gittin' tired of standin' here.

SKIP. Me too. Can't we git Lonnie Roy sworn in sittin' down? (*He sits down.*)

L.D. Hell no, Skip!

MILO. Confound it, Skip, you're gonna ruin the whole darn thing.

SKIP. Hell with it. Ah done my part. Guided old Lonnie Roy here plumb to the Mystic Mountain an' ah'm bushed. Besides that, my piles itch. (*He squirms around in the chair.*)

L.D. Goddamnit, Skip, stand up!

COLONEL. Gits goddamn dark in the trenches, ah can tell you. The rats come out in the dark and eat up ever'thin' they can git their teeth into.

RUFE. (*Sits down.*) Aw, the hell with it!

MILO. Now, come on, fellers, it won't hurt you none to stand up a little while longer so's we can git Lonnie Roy sworn in proper.

COLONEL. Them rats was fat too. Big and fat, that's 'cause there was so many bodies to eat on, you see, and the fellers used to say that if one of them rats breathed on you that you would die! That's right, they would come up at night and breathe on you, then they would commence eatin' on your body. That's right. That's right!

OLIN. Hey, Colonel, take it easy. Boy ah don't know, L.D., he's really got snakes in his boots tonight.

L.D. He'll be okay, jest leave him alone, Olin.

LONNIE. What's wrong with him? He crazy or somethin'?

L.D. No, no, of course not, he jest has these spells. Now, please, will ever'body sit down.

OLIN. Me too?

L.D. You too.

OLIN. About by-God time.

RED. (*Moving off platform.*) Ah wish to hell you'd make up your damn mind.

L.D. Well, it is made up. Ah want ever'body sittin'. (Lonnie Roy *makes a move for the chair.*)

Damnit, Lonnie Roy, not you!

LONNIE. Mah knees hurt.

L.D. Well, that's too bad. *You* gotta kneel down there.

LONNIE. Yes, sir.

SKIP. For Christ's sake, let's git this damn thing over with and have a drink!

RED. Why the hell don't you shut up, you goddamn little lush. You'll get a drink when ever'body else does and not until then!

SKIP. Ah'm not a lush, damn you, ah'm not! Who the hell do you think you're talkin' to anyway?

RED. Oh sure, ah plumb forgot. You're a hero, ain't you? A Korean war hero.

SKIP. Ah seen plenty of stuff over there, lot more than the Colonel ever seen; ah been in battles, big battles.

RED. Shore, shore. The battle of the Tattoo Parlor and the Beer Hall. Face it, Skip, you're nuthin' but a phony, a boozer and a phony.

SKIP. Ah'm not, damn you! Ah'm not!

L.D. All right now, all right, that's jest a goddamn nuff! This part I'm about to read is real important and ah want it quiet in here!

(*The cross light comes on again, this time very bright and vivid, then it goes off.*)

RUFE. Mah Gawd, did you see that!

COLONEL. What was that? What was that flash?

L.D. Nuthin', Colonel, just that damn-fool cross actin' up again.

(*Cross sputters on and off.*)

COLONEL. A creepin' barrage. *Five-nines* and *seventy-sevens*, blowin' up all around us! Throwin' up bodies of Frenchmen that was killed over a year before. Old bodies and new bodies jumbled together in the air.

SKIP. (*Getting up and moving away.*) Mah God, listen to that! For Christ's sake, somebody shut him up!

(*Cross sputters on and off.*)

COLONEL. (*His voice rising to a high whine.*) Hangin' on the old bob wire like pieces of pork. Fellers out there with half their guts shot away, sharin' a shell hole with a year-old corpse, out there all night screamin' and cryin' on the old bob wire.

RUFE. (*In a hushed voice.*) Mah God, ah ain't never heard him talk this crazy-like affore.

(*The cross light flares on and off again.*)

COLONEL. Stop that, stop doin' that! Can't you see ah'm old now? Ah'm old, ah'm an old man! Ah'm not like ah was. Ah was young then. Ah was young when ah was in France. Ah could be with wimmen. Walkin' down them streets of Bar-le-Duc like some kind of young god, American Doughboy, six foot tall. Oh, God. Oh, mah God. What's wrong with me?

SKIP. (*Going to him.*) Colonel Kinkaid? Colonel Kinkaid, for God's sake, stop it! Snap out of it!

COLONEL. Who is that? Who's got hold of me? Is that you, George?

SKIP. No, Colonel, it's . . .

COLONEL. Is that you, George Plummer? Remember when we was at the Argonne. Them dirty bastards killed you there, didn't they, George Plummer? You was afraid and that goddamned whiz-bang hit and tore off your head, and your body jumped up and run off like it was still alive, flappin' its arms and runnin' and the boys next to me shootin' at it, shootin' at it, shootin' at it for the hell of it, shootin' and laughin' and your head rollin' around on the duckboards at the bottom of the trench like some kind of ball.

SKIP. He's gone crazy, it's like he was still over there. Still fightin' that old war.

RED. Doesn't sound too heroic when it's the real thing, does it, hot shot! (*Cross sputters on and off.*)

RUFE. Maybe we better git him outta here.

L.D. Olin, you better go on down to the lobby and git Ramsey-Eyes to phone over to the Colonel's house and tell Floyd to come on over here and pick up his daddy.

OLIN. Shore thing. (*He exits. Cross sputters on and off.*)

COLONEL. Killin' people all around me! Throwin' the bodies up in the air! Up in the air.

L.D. Shore, Colonel, shore.

LONNIE. We gonna have the rest of the readin' soon?

L.D. The what? Oh, shore, shore, Lonnie Roy, of course we are.

LONNIE. Shore seems like a long time.

COLONEL. The padre come along and put that head in a sack. It musta been a flour sack or somethin', 'cause when he walked, it let out little puffs of smoke and the blood run out over his shoes and over his . . . over his puttees. One of the boys yelled out, "Hey, Padre, you're gettin' maggots in the gravy." Hey, Padre, you're gettin' mag . . . mag . . . oh, mah God!

SKIP. Jesus Christ, now that's enough. (*Backing away.*) That's enough!

RED. Maybe a shot of whiskey would help him.

L.D. Damn good idea, Red. Bring that bottle over here.

RUFE. Why don't you jest leave him be?

L.D. Ah'll hold his head back and you give him a drink.

RED. Okay. (*L.D. holds the Colonel's head back and Red puts the bottle to the Colonel's lips. The Colonel thrashes about violently and spits the fluid out all over Red's shirt.*) Look here what he done to my shirt.

COLONEL. Let me go, let me go. Ah ain't crazy, damn you! It's jest them shells. Oh, Jesus, they're comin', the Germans. Oh, Jesus God, ah can see their shadows up agin the wire.

RED. Goddamn crazy old fool, look what he done to my shirt!

OLIN. (*Entering.*) Ramsey-Eyes is phonin' over to Floyd's now.

RED. Damnit to hell, this a bran'-new shirt.

RUFE. Serves you right. Ah told you to leave him alone.

RED. Keep your damn trap shut, Rufe. Who the hell asked you anythin'.

OLIN. Now hold on here. There ain't no call for you to go yellin' at Rufe.

RED. Ah'll yell at anybody ah damn well want to!

SKIP. To hell with this, ah need a drink! (*He grabs bottle.*)

RED. Put down that bottle, Skip.

SKIP. Go to hell, ah need this!

RED. Gimme that bottle or ah'll break your goddamn neck!

SKIP. (*Pulling an object from his pocket and concealing it with his hand.*) If you think you can git by this-here knife, you jest come on ahead!

LONNIE. (*Jumping away.*) Jesus God, he's got him a knife!

L.D. Don't be a damn fool, Skip. Come on and give us the knife, then you can have all you want to drink.

SKIP. Ah got all ah want right now. (*He takes a long drink.*)

RED. You rotten little bastard! You stinkin' two-bit lush!

SKIP. Stay where you are, Red, or ah'll cut you! Ah ain't kiddin' now.

RUFE. (*Backing away.*) Watch him, Red, watch him.

MILO. Maybe we'd better adjourn this-here meetin' and finish off the initiation next time.

COLONEL. (*Grabbing hold of* Lonnie Roy, *who has backed into his wheelchair.*) Help me, help me. God in heaven, help me.

LONNIE. (*Screams and struggles to get loose.*) He's got me! He's got me! Old crazy man's got me! Old crazy man's got me, help, help. (*He tears loose from the* Colonel *and bolts out the door. The* Colonel *slumps over in his chair.*)

L.D. Stop him, Olin, don't let him get away!

OLIN. Come on, Rufe.

(*They dash out the door after* Lonnie Roy.)

RED. To hell with him. Help me git the knife away from Skip.

L.D. Come on now, Skip. Give me that knife.

SKIP. (*Hands* L.D. *a small tire gauge and grins.*) What knife?

L.D. Damn tire gauge!

RED. (*Advances on* Skip *swiftly.*) You son-of-a-bitch! (*He grabs the bottle from* Skip *and smashes him viciously in the stomach.* Skip *doubles up and falls to the floor.*)

SKIP. Oh, my gut. Damn you, Red, ah think ah'm gonna puke.

RED. (*Pulling him up.*) Not in here you ain't. (*He opens the door and pushes* Skip *out.*) Git your ass on down the hall. (Red *comes back in and closes the door.*) Half a bottle. That damn little sot drank half a bottle.

MILO. Well, ah think it's time for me to be gittin' on home now.

L.D. No! By God, you stay right where you are, Milo.

MILO. Gee, L.D., it's gittin' late and you know my mother waits up for me on meetin' nights.

L.D. Screw your mother! You're stayin' right here till Olin and Rufe git back with Lonnie Roy.

MILO. (*Shocked.*) What did you say about my mother?

L.D. Nuthin', Milo. Ah mean, ah didn't mean to say it.

MILO. You had no call to say somethin' like that. No call at all, now, by gollies, you apologize, L.D. You jest apologize for sayin' that!

RED. Go to hell! L.D. here ain't apologizin' for nuthin'.

L.D. Now wait a minute, Red . . .

MILO. Well, he better! He jest better or ah'm walkin' out that-there door an' never comin' back!

RED. Well, go ahead and walk damnit. Who the hell needs you. Stinkin' little mama's boy!

L.D. Now hold on a minute, Red. Wait, Milo, don't go.

MILO. Well, ah'm goin'. Ah'm goin' right now!

RED. You bet your ass you are. Git!!! (Milo *exits, then returns suddenly.*)

MILO. Ah never did like you, Red Grover, never You're nuthin' but a lard-butted booze drinker. (*He exits.*)

RED. (*Laughing.*) "Lard-butted booze drinker." By God, ah've been called worse.

L.D. You had no call to do that.

RED. Do what?

L.D. Treat Milo thataway.

RED. Well, hell, L.D., you're the one that told him to go hump his own mother.

L.D. Ah didn't mean that, but you did. You meant to run him off.

RED. So damn what. Ah never liked the gutless little s.o.b. anyway

L.D. But we need him. We need ever'body, don't you see? Jesus, we're breakin' up. Jest when things are startin' to look good, we start breakin' up. (Rufe *and* Olin *enter.*)

RUFE. Well, he's gone.

L.D. You couldn't catch him, huh?

OLIN. The way that boy was runnin', he's probable back in Silver City by now.

RUFE. (*Sitting down.*) Olin and me is gittin' too old to run all over Bradleyville after half-initiated kids.

OLIN. (*Seeing Colonel.*) What's wrong with the Colonel?

L.D. (*Rushing to* Colonel.) Oh, mah God! Colonel Kinkaid, are you okay? Colonel Kinkaid?

57

(Olin *and* Rufe *gather around.*)

OLIN. Is he dead?

L.D. (*Feeling* Colonel's *pulse.*) No, his heart's still beatin', but, mah God, he looks terrible. Olin, you and Rufe better git him on down to the lobby and wait with him till Floyd gits here.

RUFE. Okay, L.D. Come on, Olin. We'll wheel him to the stairs and carry him on down from there. (*He wheels the* Colonel *out the door.* L.D. *watches them for a moment and then closes the door.*)

RED. Well, sir, that about does it.

L.D. Yeah, ah guess the meetin's over all right. (*Starting to collect hats.*) Now, look here, that damn-fool Milo Crawford ran outta here with his moon hat on.

RED. No, ah don't mean the meetin'. Ah mean the whole shootin' match. There ain't gonna be any more meetin's.

L.D. You're crazy!

RED. Ah am, huh?

L.D. Yes. We ain't through by a long shot.

RED. Sure we are, L.D. That old man down there's gonna die. Ah can tell by lookin' at him, and with him dead there goes the old meetin' room. Like ah told you before, Floyd ain't gonna give nuthin' free to nobody.

L.D. So what? That don't mean nuthin'. We can meet somewheres else. Hell's fire, the brotherhood means more than jest a beat-up old room in a flea-bag hotel.

RED. The *brotherhood*? Oh, mah God! The *"brotherhood!"* Jesus Christ, L.D., wake up. Git back on the goddamn planet. The *brotherhood* ain't any more. The *brotherhood* ran outta here with Lonnie Roy and Milo. The *brotherhood* fell on its ass with Skip over there. The *brotherhood* got carried outta here with a dyin' old man. There ain't gonna be no stinkin' Knights of the White Magnolia cause the Knights of the White Magnolia idea is gone, finished, all washed up. Did you really listen to that crap we were readin' tonight? The Gospel according to Maynard C. Stempco. The sun, the moon, and the west wind? Well, L.D., old pal, lemme tell you as far as this-here lodge is concerned, the sun's done set, the moon's gone down, and the west wind's got a big splotch on it.

L.D. That ain't true! The ideas that this-here lodge was founded on have a hell of a lot of meanin'.

RED. Meanin'? Meanin' to who? For God's sake, take a look around you, L.D., whatta ya see? Domino players, stumble bums, mama's boys, pimple-faced kids, and crazy old men.

L.D. And you? Just where the hell do you fit in?

RED. Me? Ah don't fit in nowhere. Ah'm just a lard-butted booze drinker. Remember? (*He picks up the sack of whiskey.*) So I guess that jest leaves you, L.D. The only true believer, L. D. Alexander, supermarket manager and keeper of the White Magnolias. Let me tell you somethin', Brother White Knight, Imperial Wizard, you don't put down the sons-of-bitchin' freedom riders and minority bastards with all this crap any more. You got to look for the loopholes, pal. Let 'em all squawk about lunchrooms and schools all they want. In mah place ah simply reserve the right to refuse service to anybody. You look for the loopholes, pal. Well, so long, L.D. If ah don't see you down to the bar, ah'll save a seat for you on the back of the bus. (*He pitches the half-empty pint to him and exits, leaving the door open. L.D. watches him off and glances dejectedly around. Crosses to the door and closes it, then to the Stempco portrait and contemplates a moment, then he crosses to the truth banner, and after a moment rips it down and tosses it into the trunk. He takes off his hat and throws it into the trunk as well. The sound of a train passing through town makes him pause. The door opens and Skip comes in.*)

SKIP. Jesus, ah think he busted mah gut. Ah been pukin' up Dixie Dinette chiliburgers by the goddamn bucketful.

L.D. (*Giving Skip the bottle.*) Here, maybe this will help.

SKIP. Oh, God, thanks. (*He drinks.*) Where the hell is ever'body?

L.D. Gone.

SKIP. Gone? Gone where?

L.D. Quit. Walked out.

SKIP. Quit? Who quit?

L.D. Lonnie Roy, Milo, and Red.

SKIP. What about the rest of the guys?

L.D. Finished. It's all finished.

SKIP. (*Getting up.*) You mean Colonel Kinkaid quit too?

L.D. You might say so, yes.

SKIP. Well, ah'll be damned.

(Olin *and* Rufe *re-enter.*)

RUFE. Well, Floyd finally got here.

OLIN. He said he was gonna take his daddy straight over to Doc Crowley's. He was mad as hell at us for lettin' the Colonel get into that shape.

RUFE. That's right. He says he's gonna shut down the meetin' room.

L.D. Let him go ahead. It don't matter no more anyway.

OLIN. Well, hell, L.D., if we cain't come up here no more, where we gonna hold our meetin's?

L.D. Whattayou care? What the hell do you come to the meetin's for anyway?

OLIN. Well, hell, L.D., me and Rufe like to play the domino games and Skip there, he, well, uh . . .

L.D. Shore, shore, we all know why Skip comes up here.

SKIP. Now wait a minute. Ah never done nuthin'.

RUFE. Well, hell, L.D., we cain't jest quit.

L.D. Who says we cain't? Ah'm tired of tryin' to keep ever'thin' goin' any more. Watchin', things bust apart. Things aint the same no more. Damn, damn, things is changin'. Damn. Oh, to hell with it. (*He walks to the podium and picks up the initiation book.*) This-here lodge, this-here society, this-here brotherhood, this-here ever'thin' is now adjourned! (*He takes the book and slowly walks out.*)

OLIN. Well, what the hell do you think about that?

RUFE. What did he mean, "This-here brotherhood is now adjourned"?

SKIP. Ah think we jest knighted our last Magnolia, boys. All the rest of the brothers done flew the coop.

RUFE. You mean that we're all the members there is?

SKIP. That's right. Who would have thought that one day old Olin Potts there would be the Grand Imperial Wizard of the White Magnolia? Stempco! Stempco! Stempco!

RUFE. Doggone it, ah'm sure gonna miss our old meetin' nights.

SKIP. Oh hell, yes, me too. Especially this last one. (*He rubs his stomach.*)

RUFE. Now there won't be nuthin' to do.

OLIN. Aw hell, Rufe, there's always somethin' to do. We could go over there to the new bowlin' alley and give that a try.

RUFE. Yeah, I spoze we could. Well, ah gotta be gittin' on back home now or Sara Beth will be mad as hell.

OLIN. Not half as mad as old Mabel's gonna be at me.

RUFE. What the hell you talkin' about, Olin? You know damn well Sara Beth can git a hunred times madder than Mabel ever could.

OLIN. Now listen here, Rufe Phelps, that ain't true.

RUFE. The hell it ain't. Old Sara Beth gits up in the morning mad at the rooster an' goes to bed at night cussin' the owl.

(*They exit arguing. Skip watches the exit and finishes the rest of the bottle. He flips the bottle cap. Ramsey-Eyes enters.*)

RAMSEY-EYES. Meetin' all over with, Mistah Skip?

SKIP. Yes, Ramsey-Eyes, the meetin' is all over.

RAMSEY-EYES. Ah'll jest straighten thangs up and lock de door.

SKIP. You jest do that little old thing. Ramsey-Eyes. (*He looks at the empty bottle.*) Christ, ah wish ah had another drink.

RAMSEY-EYES. Mistah Red Grover is over to his saloon. Ah seed him go over dere when he left the hotel here.

SKIP. Hot damn! Ah'll bet he'll give me a drink, sure enough, ah jest bet he will. Thanks, Ramsey-Eyes. Good night. (*He exits.*)

RAMSEY-EYES. Good night, Mistah Skip. (*He closes the door and snaps the cross light switch a couple of times. When it doesn't work, he moves to the cross and raps the wall next to it with the broom handle. The cross lights up. He chuckles and moves back to the door, turning off the overhead lights. A piece of paper catches his eye. He picks it up and moves to the light of the cross to read.*) "Ah am de moon. By night ah cast beams down upon you, lightin' your way along your journey toward de truth." (*He chuckles.*) "Ah am de moon." Oh, Lawdy. "Ah am de moon." (*He chuckles again. The cross lights fade to blackout.*)

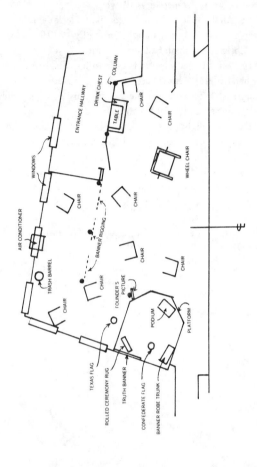

SCENE DESIGN

"The Last Meeting of the Knights of the White Magnolia"
As Designed by Ben Edwards, for the Washington, D.C.
and New York Productions (Proscenium Stage)

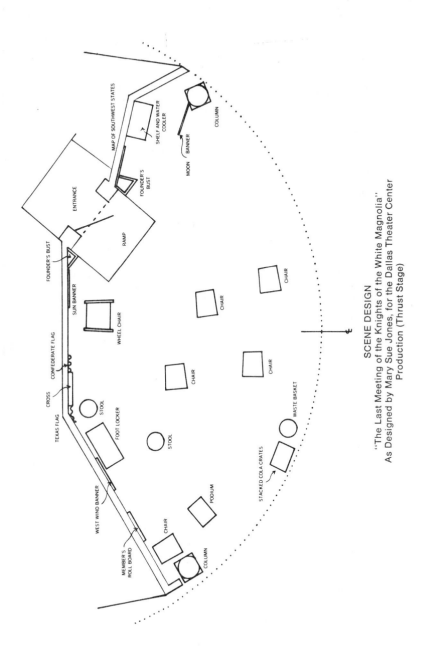

SCENE DESIGN
"The Last Meeting of the Knights of the White Magnolia"
As Designed by Mary Sue Jones, for the Dallas Theater Center
Production (Thrust Stage)

PROPERTY LIST

On Stage
    Assorted, battered chairs
    Old wheelchair, with lap robe
    Framed portrait of "Maynard C. Stempco" on wall
    Small podium, on low platform, with white magnolia painted on it
    Two flags: "The Stars and Bars" and "Lone Star" behind podium
    Cross made of light bulbs, between flags
    Coat rack, on U. wall
    Old trunk, with initiation hats, on floor by coat rack
    Old banners representing the sun, the moon and the west wind, on
        U. and L. walls
    Broom (Ramsey-Eyes)

Off Stage
    Paper bag, with 4 bottles of bourbon (Red)
    Initiation book, with cards in it (Olin)

Personal
    Tire gauge (Skip)

NEW PLAYS

- **SMASH by Jeffrey Hatcher.** Based on the novel, AN UNSOCIAL SOCIALIST by George Bernard Shaw, the story centers on a millionaire Socialist who leaves his bride on their wedding day because he fears his passion for her will get in the way of his plans to overthrow the British government. *"SMASH is witty, cunning, intelligent, and skillful."* –*Seattle Weekly*. *"SMASH is a wonderfully high-style British comedy of manners that evokes the world of Shaw's high-minded heroes and heroines, but shaped by a post modern sensibility."* –*Seattle Herald*. [5M, 5W] ISBN: 0-8222-1553-5

- **PRIVATE EYES by Steven Dietz.** A comedy of suspicion in which nothing is ever quite what it seems. *"Steven Dietz's ... Pirandellian smooch to the mercurial nature of theatrical illusion and romantic truth, Dietz's spiraling structure and breathless pacing provide enough of an oxygen rush to revive any moribund audience member ... Dietz's mastery of playmaking ... is cause for kudos."* –*The Village Voice*. *"The cleverest and most artful piece presented at the 21st annual [Humana] festival was PRIVATE EYES by writer-director Steven Dietz."* –*The Chicago Tribune*. [3M, 2W] ISBN: 0-8222-1619-1

- **DIMLY PERCEIVED THREATS TO THE SYSTEM by Jon Klein.** Reality and fantasy overlap with hilarious results as this unforgettable family attempts to survive the nineties. *"Here's a play whose point about fractured families goes to the heart, mind -- and ears."* –*The Washington Post*. *" ... an end-of-the millennium comedy about a family on the verge of a nervous breakdown ... Trenchant and hilarious ... "* –*The Baltimore Sun*. [2M, 4W] ISBN: 0-8222-1677-9

- **HONOUR by Joanna Murray-Smith.** In a series of intense confrontations, a wife, husband, lover and daughter negotiate the forces of passion, lust, history, responsibility and honour. *"Tight, crackling dialogue (usually played out in punchy verbal duels) captures characters unable to deal with emotions ... Murray-Smith effectively places her characters in situations that strip away pretense."* –*Variety*. *"HONOUR might just capture a few honors of its own."* –*Time Out Magazine*. [1M, 3W] ISBN: 0-8222-1683-3

- **NINE ARMENIANS by Leslie Ayvazian.** A revealing portrait of three generations of an Armenian-American family. *" ... Ayvazian's obvious personal exploration ... is evocative, and her picture of an American Life colored nostalgically by an increasingly alien ethnic tradition, is persuasively embedded into a script of a certain supple grace ... "* –*The NY Post*. *"... NINE ARMENIANS is a warm, likable work that benefits from ... Ayvazian's clear-headed insight into the dynamics of a close-knit family ... "* –*Variety*. [5M, 5W] ISBN: 0-8222-1602-7

- **PSYCHOPATHIA SEXUALIS by John Patrick Shanley.** Fetishes and psychiatry abound in this scathing comedy about a man and his father's argyle socks. *"John Patrick Shanley's new play, PSYCHOPATHIA SEXUALIS is ... perfectly poised between daffy comedy and believable human neurosis which Shanley combines so well ... "* –*The LA Times*. *"John Patrick Shanley's PSYCHOPATHIA SEXUALIS is a salty boulevard comedy with a bittersweet theme ... "* –*New York Magazine*. *"A tour de force of witty, barbed dialogue."* –*Variety*. [3M, 2W] ISBN: 0-8222-1615-9

DRAMATISTS PLAY SERVICE, INC.
440 Park Avenue South, New York, NY 10016 212-683-8960 Fax 212-213-1539
postmaster@dramatists.com www.dramatists.com

NEW PLAYS

• **A QUESTION OF MERCY by David Rabe.** The Obie Award-winning playwright probes the sensitive and controversial issue of doctor-assisted suicide in the age of AIDS in this poignant drama. *"There are many devastating ironies in Mr. Rabe's beautifully considered, piercingly clear-eyed work ... " –The NY Times. "With unsettling candor and disturbing insight, the play arouses pity and understanding of a troubling subject ... Rabe's provocative tale is an affirmation of dignity that rings clear and true." –Variety.* [6M, 1W] ISBN: 0-8222-1643-4

• **A DOLL'S HOUSE by Henrik Ibsen, adapted by Frank McGuinness. Winner of the 1997 Tony Award for best revival.** *"New, raw, gut-twisting and gripping. Easily the hottest drama this season." –USA Today. "Bold, brilliant and alive." –The Wall Street Journal. "A thunderclap of an evening that takes your breath away." –Time. "The stuff of Broadway legend." –Associated Press.* [4M, 4W, 2 boys] ISBN: 0-8222-1636-1

• **THE WAITING ROOM by Lisa Loomer.** Three women from different centuries meet in a doctor's waiting room in this dark comedy about the timeless quest for beauty -- and its cost. *" ... THE WAITING ROOM ... is a bold, risky melange of conflicting elements that is ... terrifically moving ... There's no resisting the fierce emotional pull of the play." – The NY Times. " ... one of the high points of this year's Off-Broadway season ... THE WAITING ROOM is well worth a visit." –Back Stage.* [7M, 4W, flexible casting] ISBN: 0-8222-1594-2

• **MR. PETERS' CONNECTIONS by Arthur Miller.** Mr. Miller describes the protagonist as existing in a dream-like state when the mind is "freed to roam from real memories to conjectures, from trivialities to tragic insights, from terror of death to glorying in one's being alive." With this memory play, the Tony Award and Pulitzer Prize-winner reaffirms his stature as the world's foremost dramatist. *" ... a cross between Joycean stream-of-consciousness and Strindberg's dream plays, sweetened with a dose of William Saroyan's philosophical whimsy ... CONNECTIONS is most intriguing ... Miller scholars will surely find many connections of their own to make between this work and the author's earlier plays." –The NY Times.* [5M, 3W] ISBN: 0-8222-1687-6

• **THE STEWARD OF CHRISTENDOM by Sebastian Barry.** A freely imagined portrait of the author's great-grandfather, the last Chief Superintendent of the Dublin Metropolitan Police. *"MAGNIFICENT ... the cool, elegiac eye of James Joyce's THE DEAD; the bleak absurdity of Samuel Beckett's lost, primal characters; the cosmic anger of KING LEAR ..." –The NY Times. "Sebastian Barry's compassionate imaging of an ancestor he never knew is among the most poignant onstage displays of humanity in recent memory." –Variety.* [5M, 4W] ISBN: 0-8222-1609-4

• **SYMPATHETIC MAGIC by Lanford Wilson. Winner of the 1997 Obie for best play.** The mysteries of the universe, and of human and artistic creation, are explored in this award-winning play. *"Lanford Wilson's idiosyncratic SYMPATHETIC MAGIC is his BEST PLAY YET ... the rare play you WANT ... chock-full of ideas, incidents, witty or poetic lines, scientific and philosophical argument ... you'll find your intellectual faculties racing." – New York Magazine. "The script is like a fully notated score, next to which most new plays are cursory lead sheets." –The Village Voice.* [5M, 3W] ISBN: 0-8222-1630-2

DRAMATISTS PLAY SERVICE, INC.
440 Park Avenue South, New York, NY 10016 212-683-8960 Fax 212-213-1539
postmaster@dramatists.com www.dramatists.com